WELCOME TO ST ROQUES

**Illustrated Short Tall Stories
By
J.P. O'Day
Includes Illustrated Dundee
Dictionary**

Copyright © J.P. O'Day 2014 All rights reserved

ISBN 978-1499308310

Cover illustration: Abandon all soap, ye who enter here.
Illustrations by Derek A Thomson

Intro

**Had I lived among ancient Greeks,
They'd garland me with Laurels,
But here I'm wearing cast aff breeks,
And living on cald Farrels.**

McGonagall (i think)

The tales in this collection are mainly set during the 1950s in a triangle of streets in the east of Dundee: Blackscroft, Peep O' Day Lane and Foundry Lane. At one time the area had been known as St Roques, hence the name of the Library, and St Roques Lane, aka the **shitey pend**. The significance of St Roque to the area is a bit of a mystery, but he is invoked for diseases, especially skin diseases. The area is outside where the old city walls would have been, and it seems it was used as a leper colony at one time, and no doubt sufferers of the Black Death would have been confined there. Some of the older folk in the area, like my Granddad who was born there, did refer to it as the Rokie.

The Rokie had been a fairly thriving place at one time, with as much as a thousand folk staying in the various two, three and four storey tenements and odd cottages and houses. There was also a few old, small factories, mills and workshops, and Foundry Lane itself took its name from the Foundry that was still there and still working in the 50s, though not on the same scale that it once had. By the time I lived there in the 50s however, there was probably only about a hundred and odd people living there. Although the folk who lived there, or at least some of them, tried to keep the place clean, there was a sense of decay about the Rokie. The buildings were grimy and had been neglected for years, burst pipes and broken windows were not repaired and piles of rubbish rotted in the backies and corners. For those who still lived there however, life went on.

Blackscroft was still pretty much as it had always been. The only changes in my time there were a row of tenements and a row of old cottages on the south side of the street had been demolished, and billboards advertising the usual soap powder and the like, put up to cover the gaps they left. The tenements that were left were of the usual three and four storeys, with the ground floors being occupied by shops, most of which were disused. Behind the buildings on the north side of Blackscroft were warehouses and small workshops, mainly belonging to Halley's jute mill.

Peep o' Day Lane Lane was exactly as it always had been though. There were only ever three buildings on the lane, two on the west side: a four storey tenement, and an old day school on the corner with Foundry Lane. The school belonged to St Mary's Church, part of the Old Steeple, and was used for such as the BB, and was known locally as the Kirky. On the east side of the Lane was the imposing, high stone wall of the giant Gasworks. At the top of the Lane on the east side, the council had built a men's toilet, the front of which was part of the Gasworks wall.

Foundry Lane was the same, with buildings only on one side, and the wall of the city Coalyards on the other. Apart from the Foundry that gave the

Lane its name, and the old day school on the corner of Peep o' Day Lane, there was only one tenement, a few old cottages and a couple of empty workshops still standing. There were a few gaps where the buildings had been knocked down, no point in billboards when there was nobody to see them. So these gaps were just left to the dogs, the rats and the bairns to play on. Somebody had even fenced off one gap site and kept a horse there, but nobody seemed to know who.

At some time in the past, the folk in the Rokie had got together, and after much deliberation, decided to call the Gasworks and the Coalyards, the **Gassy** and the **Coaly.** The Gassy and the Coaly lay to the east and south of St Roques, while Halley's mills and warehouses lay to the north. This gave the Rokie a feel of being cut off and hidden from the rest of the city. Sort of like an island in an industrial sea that lay outside the triangle of streets.

Inside the triangle of streets, there was a labyrinth of pends, alleys, stairways and Closes. These all led to other cottages, small workshops and the like. Some of these were still occupied, while some lay empty and boarded up. Some of the empty ones that weren't boarded up sat with doors lying open and windows all broken. Sometimes a tramp would take up temporary residence, especially over the winter months, and a couple of pigeon fanciers used them for lofts. Generally though, the empty houses and the like were used by the bairns, especially laddies, for playing Japs and British, Cowsers and the like.

Behind the billboards that ran along Blackscroft from the top of Peep O' Day Lane, there was a bit of disused ground where some whalers cottages had been at one time. On this ground sat the Labour Hall, which was just a very large wooden hut. The ground was a good bit higher than where our tenement sat, so access to it could be gained by climbing up a wall at the back of our Close. This ground was a paradise for us bairns. We constantly played all sorts of games in the nooks and crannies and long grass of what was known as the Hutty.

I lived in a typical Dundee tenement of the time. It had four floors with four two roomed houses on each floor. The houses were reached by a common Close to a turret stairway which was built off the back of the building, then by means of a verandah to each house. These verandahs have forever been known in Dundee as Plettys. I lived in one of the houses on the third floor. Due to lack of space, I lived with my Gran and Granddad, while my mother lived upstairs with my stepdad, Eddie, and two wee half-brothers Davy and Tam. Also upstairs, were one of my mother's sisters, my auntie Jean, along with my uncle Dode and cousins wee Dode and Ronnie. Downstairs on the first floor, my Granddads two sisters, my great-aunties, lived together in one of the houses.

Having my wee brothers and cousins in the same land meant an instant gang. I was the oldest, while wee Dode was a year younger, with Ronnie and Davy being a year younger again. Tam was a good bit younger, so though he was generally around, he tended to play with the other younger bairns. Sometimes, our playgrounds were the streets in the Rokie, which were usually devoid of traffic and had no cars at all parked in the three streets. Occasionally we would go to the swing park on Blackscroft, but we found the swings pretty boring and generally just full of wee lassies. Our main places for games and mischief though, were the Hutty and our own backies. At the back of our Close, there was a gap between the Close and the stair turret. The right side led out to the backies, while the left side led to a short Pletty. The houses on the ground floor had their doors off the Close, so this Pletty didn't lead anywhere. However, a few of the railings on it had been broken off years ago, and so for us bairns also led out to the backies. Also on this Pletty was the boaly, which was the space under the stairs. The boaly was a dark space about eight feet deep, with a ceiling that sloped down as it went back. We used the boaly for sitting in on rainy days when the washouse was being used or locked up. At nights, it was so dark we never went near it. In fact we were sure it was haunted, hence the term, the boaly Ghost. I had found a loose brick in the wall of the boaly, and found that there was a small space behind it, this was my posy hole for secret stuff like bangers and nood books.

We were in a house on the end of the third floor Pletty and shared the outside toilet with eighteen other people on weekdays, and sixteen at the weekends and holidays. The reason for this was quite simple, the house at the other end of the Pletty was occupied by a man and his wife and their seven children, but they also had two lodgers who worked on the night shift at the nearby shipyard. They worked there on weeknights, and slept during the day when the beds were unoccupied. The two lodgers were brothers who came from a town some distance away. They only came into the city to work and went home at the weekends and holidays.

By the time these tales are set, nearly all the shops on Blackscroft had closed and were lying empty, with some boarded up. The only survivors were: Harry Bradley's pub, the Pawn shop, a Newsagents, Tyree's Bakery, Robertson's Grocery, Fureys junk shop, a second hand furniture shop, a shop that had bacon slicers and scales and the like in the window, but was never open, and a nood book shop. The owners of these shops didn't kid themselves on, they knew it was just a matter of time before everybody else left and they too would have to give up the Ghost. But most had been there so long they just decided to hang on as long as possible.

The only building of any note in the Rokie was the local Library. This building had obviously had no expense spared on it, and had been built in the Classical Greek style. At either side of the main door there were stone columns, and the door itself wouldn't be out of place on the front of Buckingham Palace, while the windows were of stained glass depicting great scientific and literary figures. The garden in front of the Library had obviously been put together with the idea of contemplation and serious study in mind. There were benches situated under Lilac trees and surrounded by scented shrubs, and there were stone busts and reliefs of scholarly figures such as Plato and Newton. This philosophical atmosphere was not lost on the users of the Library either, and on days when the weather permitted, it was not unusual to see several people sitting reading the latest Durango Kid or Mickey Spillane story in the company of an approving Socrates and a bottle of Pineappleade.

So, that was the scenario for the tales in this collection. There were also some amazing characters, and the following pages give an outline before the stories begin. For anyone struggling with words in the Dundee accent, there is a dictionary following the stories.

My Gran and Granddad

Frankie McPhee: Probably the dirtiest person who ever lived.

Harry Bradley: Owner of the only pub in the Rokie.

Sticky Tam: Local wit and seller of firewood.

Slaberee Alec: The local Boabee.

Obvious Joe: Probably the stupidest person who ever lived.

Dan Doogan: Local whisky distiller, bottler and supplier.

Lenny Black: Local street bookie and all round villain.

Daft Tam: Local drunk

Daft Johnny: Backward lad who lived with and worked for Sticky Tam.

Louie the Next: Self employed bespoke tailor.

My Gran and Granddad had lived in their house since they had married umpteen years ago. They had brought up their own six bairns in the house, who had now all left and had families of their own, except my uncle John who was nearly always at sea.

My Granddad worked as the lodge man at the big sawmills down at the docks. Basically, he kept all the men's time cards up to date, sounded the siren for start and finish work and did various odd jobs. My Gran also worked at the sawmills part time as the office cleaner. They never earned much money for either job, but both being of simple tastes, they managed along fine, and in some cases better than most. The house didn't have much in the way of furniture, but what was there was of pretty good quality and had lasted them most of there married lives. Which was about how long it had taken them to pay it off. The food we ate was always of the plain kind, but it was wholesome and always home cooked. Vegetables were never a problem, as Granddad had an allotment where he grew most of what we needed.

This allotment of Granddad's wasn't really what was meant to be an allotment. At the start of the Second World War, the Dig for Victory campaign had started. The ground known as the Hutty was just lying there doing nothing, and so Granddad decided to start digging for victory. It took a lot of work to clear a small piece of the ground, but within a few weeks he had managed to get the first of his crops planted. When the war was over, nobody said he couldn't use the ground anymore, so he just kept using it as an allotment. Apart from his work, this was where Granddad spent most of his spare time. If he wasn't working on the garden, he would be chopping logs or making bits and pieces out of wood he had purloined from the sawmill. A lot of the time however, was spent just sitting and blethering to anybody who happened to drop in. This, along with his job as a lodgeman, meant my Granddad was well known in the area. I spent a lot of time with him, which was how I managed to come by the stories.

Most days and nights, Slaberee Alec, who was the local beat Boabee for the Rokie and the general harbour area, could be seen round the Rokie. His nickname came about through his face and tunic being constantly splattered with a variety of foodstuffs. This was due to his habit of constantly mooching pies, cakes, chips, sweeties, in fact anything edible. Alec was one of the old school of Boabees who had joined the force in the days when Boabees were carefully selected according to the size of their feet. He had originally came from some remote hole in the country where he was a ploughman. Changes on the land had seen many of these farm workers moving into the towns looking for work, and what better job for a semi-literate, barrel chested, six footer who was as strong as a plough horse, thick as the shite round its arse, and good with his fists.

Although he got called Daft Tam, Tam Anderson wasn't really all that daft, just a bit thick. I once asked my Granddad why Tam got called daft Tam, and he said it was just because he looked like he was daft. This was very true, Tam did in fact look like he was as daft as a brush. He always got his hair cut as short as possible, near enough shaved into the wood. Tam didn't have what you would call big ears, but they did stick out at right angles to his head, so along with his cropped hair, they were very noticeable. Like most folk, Tam's teeth had fell out at a young age, and he just couldn't be arsed with fahlsers, as he said, he didn't eat that much anyway. So this meant that there wasn't much of a gap between his chin and his nose. So, with his toothless mouth pulling his chin up towards his nose, his cropped head and stick out ears, the Three Stoogies wouldn't have to worry about a replacement if one of them suddenly dropped dead. To say that Tam liked a drink, was like saying Frankie McPhee didn't like soap. Unlike most hard drinkers however, Tam stuck to beer. Most nights he could be found in Harry Bradley's downing pint after pint of 80/- ale, which was his only tipple.

Dan Doogan was the owner of the local distillery. Not only the owner, but also the distiller, bottler, marketing director, salesman and distributor. Dan was a big man, tall, with broad shoulders and arms and a belly that proved he was no teetotaller. But Dan's most noticeable feature, was that despite being bald headed, he was possibly the hairiest man who ever lived. He was absolutely covered in thick, black hair. It was said that Dan once went to the zoo and the monkeys threw bananas at him, and one time he went for a swim in the docks, somebody phoned the Boabees to ask if there was a circus in town and were they missing something. Like what? The Boabees said. They weren't sure, was the reply, but it wears specs and its swimming about in the docks. But, that's was just what folk said. By far though, Dan's hairiest feature were his forearms and hands. His hands, or rather one of them, was a bit of a byword in the Rokie.

Frankie McPhee was reckoned to be the dirtiest person who ever lived. This wasn't something that had been arrived at by supposition. The crowd in Harry Bradley's had only arrived at this conclusion after long and careful deliberation. Witnesses had been called, and evidence had been thoroughly scrutinised before Frankie had been awarded his title. Not only was he declared the dirtiest person who ever lived, but it was also reckoned that if life was ever found on another planet, it was a fair bet Frankie would be dirtier than anyone who had ever lived there as well. Frankie's reaction to this dubious award though, was just to tell those involved to go and keech up a Closie.

In the street behind Blackscroft, in what looked like a bit of wasteground, there was a derelict cottage with a yard and a big, rusty, corrugated iron shed. This was the home and workplace of T. Christy. Firewood Merchant, also known as Sticky Tam. Tam's business was quite simple, every so often he would borrow Eck McLaren's coal lorry and head off into the country and up the coast. He would go round the farms and the harbours at the fishing towns and buy up all the old tattie and fish boxes he could find, not coming back till he had a full load. The boxes would be broken up, and then chopped up into kindling which would be tied up in manageable bunches. The bunches would then be taken in a barrow and sold door to door, or to various shops outside the Rokie. Tam was also a bit of a wit, and loved nothing better than a good joke and a laugh.

Daft Johnny had worked for Sticky Tam since he was about ten years old. It had all started when Tam had been on his rounds one night and Johnny had started following him and his cart. Eventually, Tam had sent him up Closes chapping doors with bundles of sticks. Ever since, Johnny could be seen in the company of Tam as he went round selling his stuff. In return, Tam would buy Johnny ice lollies, bottles of Pineappleade, chips and occasionally pay him into the show or give him the money to go. Although Tam benefited most from this arrangement, it also suited Johnny, and was in fact very beneficial to him in the long run. Johnny was called daft Johnny simply because he was in fact daft, not because he was mad like daft Margaret. Johnny had spent the first sixteen years of his life in the old gothic orphanage way out the Ferry road, and had come to live in the Rokie via the good will of Sticky Tam. Johnny never ever knew who his Mother and father were, he wasn't even sure if he was an orphan. All he knew, was that he had been left on the doorstep of the orphanage on the day he was born wrapped up in a Sunday Post. When he told Sticky Tam about this, Tam just said that at least he had something to read while he waited to be found.

At the foot of the Close between Harry Bradley's and the Pawn Shop, there was a small white sign on the wall. The sign said in black letters that one floor up, on the right, directly above the Pawn Shop, was the premises of Louie Nathan, Bespoke Tailor. These premises were also the home of the said Louie Nathan, known locally as Louie the Next. Louie did in fact have three dreams that he told my Granddad about.

Obvious Joe was a fat, smelly, gormless little man who had lived in the Rokie since his mother made the mistake of bringing him home after giving birth to him. He got his name just because of his habit of always saying what was blatantly obvious. It just didn't matter what anybody was doing, he had to ask them. If somebody was standing at the bus stop, Joe had to go up to them, nod his head at the bus stop, and say: ***Standing at the bus stop?*** If you were reading the paper: ***Reading the paper?*** Every day in Harry Bradley's the air was filled with: ***drinking a pint? Playing dominoes? Smoking a fag?*** It was useless trying to be sarcastic with Joe as well, retorts like:

No, I'm playing the cello or: ***No, I'm laying a roll of lino*** were totally lost on Joe, and usually just brought the response ***Are you?*** and a quick look round for the cello or lino. He very rarely ever said anything else, unless it was some earth shattering news that he had to share with the world, like the time he found a used match on the pavement. Joe could be seen most days in Harry Bradley's. He didn't drink, he just went there every day for something to do. Harry just put up with him as he was handy for the likes of collecting glasses, sweeping up and going the odd message.

In between the nood book shop and the pub, there was a Close which was the entrance to the flats above and out to the back of the building. The foot of the Close was the business premises of local entrepreneur, Lenny Black. Every day, except Sunday, no matter what the weather, Lenny would be standing there conducting business. This business consisted of taking bets on the horses, dogs, football, boxing, in fact anything. Lenny also lent money, but this was only to people who wanted money for betting. Lenny also had other business interests, but he only ran the bookies and money lending from the foot of the Close.

Like most communities, the place where more went on than any other, was the pub. This was where folk met to discuss the important issues of the day, such as who done what, what they got, or what they were going to get. The pub was where deals were done, money was lent and borrowed, plotting and planning was carried out, in fact the place where more or less everything happened.

In the Rokie, there was one pub left open when I was around, Harry Bradley's. Harry Bradley's was one of those pubs that had old fashioned swing doors just behind the main door. Like most pubs in these days, swing doors were there for a reason. Basically, it meant that they were permanently closed. As soon as someone went through them, they just swung shut again on their own. A common misconception was that this was simply to keep out the cold, but drinking, and especially in pubs, was always looked on as something that only the rough, lower classes did, and so the doors were designed to keep it, as it were, behind closed doors. This way, any decent, middle class person walking past wouldn't be confronted with the horrific, nightmare inducing, life threatening sight of someone drinking a pint. Nor would any children be corrupted into thinking that drinking was a normal, everyday kind of thing. Whether this was ever an official, legal issue, who knows. Doubt if there ever was a Swing Doors Act put through Parliament, but given the puritanical, petty mindedness of the institutions of this country, don't rule it out.

Still, permanently Closed doors on a pub had their uses. They did help on winter nights for keeping the cold out, and it was easier to get through them when carrying something. But most useful of all, it was easier to get a quarrelsome drunk out of the pub through swing doors than through an ordinary door. And of that there was never a shortage in Harry Bradley's. There were probably more drunks got chucked through Harry Bradley's swing doors than in all of John Wayne's films put together.

The pub itself consisted of only a bar and a boaly. The bar took up an area around 14 feet wide by 30 feet or so deep, in fact the same size as the houses on the floors above. But the space taken up by the bar, the toilet and the boaly reduced the actual customer area to around half of that. Yes, toilet, another way that women were discouraged from entering the male dominated world of the pub, was the fact that there was only one toilet. The old wifeys who used the boaly either had to hold it in or go home.

The pub was simply decorated, usually every five years or so with just a quite plain wallpaper of unknown colour. This was due to the fact that within a matter of no time after being put up, it was deeply stained with nicotine and turned a darker and darker brown till even the pattern disappeared. The floor was covered in linoleum simply because it was easier to clean the fag ash and ends, spilt beer and occasional blood than any other surface. There were a couple of framed photos of unknown origin on the walls, Joe Louis was there, as was Louis Armstrong and Victor Mature as Samson. There was also a framed, signed photo of Davy Crocket that Sticky Tam had brought in years before. Nobody had questioned its authenticity, but the portrait did bear a resemblance to Fess Parker, a third rate actor who had in fact played Davy Crocket in a film. The rest were photos of forgotten football players, sportsmen and the like. The pub was in fact quite a homely like place, made all the more so by the ever burning coal fire in the wall across from the bar. The fire was not only the source of heating for the pub, like all domestic and pub fires it was also the main ashtray and place where nearly all the rubbish went, and also the place the occasional drunk fell into.

A place to plot and plan

In common with other pubs too, the drinks available were minimal in Harry Bradley's. There was light and heavy draught beer, bottled beer consisted of pale ale and sweet stout, while the only spirits available were whisky and rum, that was it. Requests for such as Lager, Guiness or Vodka were usually met with derision and comments like: away to Ireland or Russia. Any request as to food was met with the information that there was a Bakers and a Chipper down the road. Food in fact could be available at certain times. Jimmy James, a local midget, came round the pubs every day at dinnertime and at teatime with a hotbox of pies, sausage rolls and bridies fresh from old man Tyree's Bakery. If he was missed, the idiot, Obvious Joe, could be sent down to the bakers. But this meant writing out a note, as Joe just couldn't be trusted to remember an order as complicated as: one pie.

There was a TV set in Harry's, but the volume was usually kept off unless something really good or important came on. This included such as: football, boxing, a cowboy, war or cops and robbers film. The only programmes that were never missed and where hushed voices had to be observed, were the news, the football results on Saturday, and the Lone Ranger. This went especially for the Lone Ranger. Apart from the TV, the entertainment in Harry's consisted entirely of dominoes, and the usual fights. There had been sing songs on Friday and Saturday nights at one time, but Harry had stopped them, but that's another story.

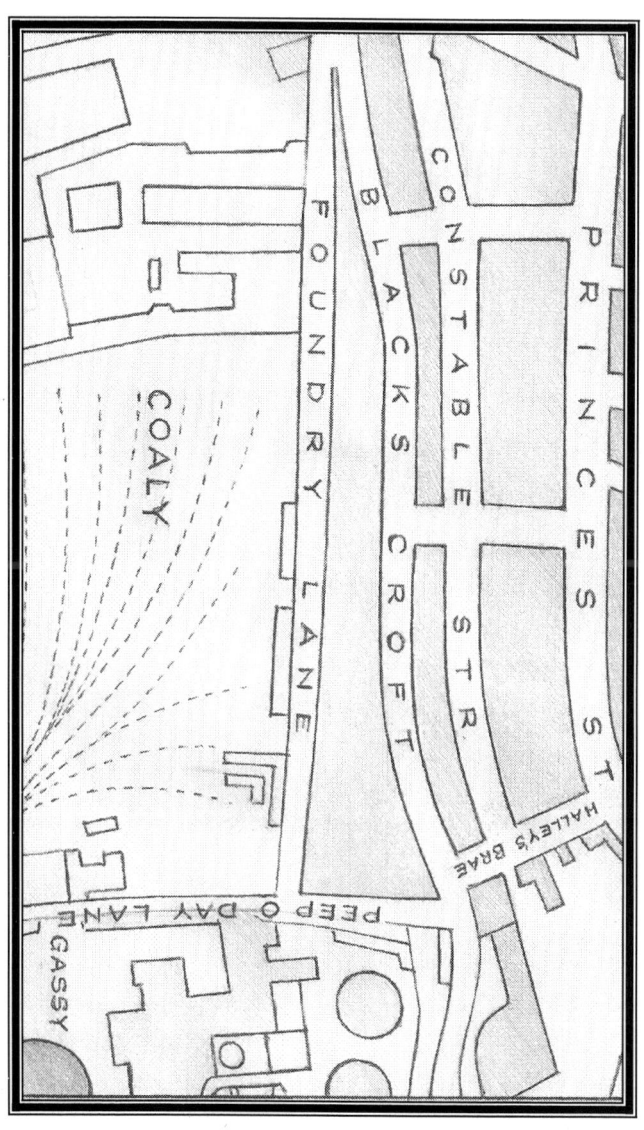

I

So, there it is, I meet a famous person.

Having nothing to do on a wet afternoon, as somebody once said, I started wandering aimlessly, jumping in dubs, standing under leaking gutters getting soaked from the torrents of water that came down, the usual stuff to do when there's nothing else. I had a look in at the Arcade, but having no money I just watched a couple of people playing the crane machine. The boy playing it was on his fifth attempt at the packet of twenty Woodbine, when Martin Luther King came in. He came over to the crane machine and asked if anybody had change of a bob. We directed him to the change booth, where he went, and then left.

When I got home, my Granddad asked what I'd been doing all day, to which I just said, nothing really, but I did meet Martin Luther King at the Arcade. My Gran just said I was havering a lot of shite, while my Granddad just asked what made me think it was him. I said it was because he was black. Granddad then asked if I was sure it wasn't just Frankie McPhee.

One day, a poster appeared on the billboards in Blackscroft. Not just any poster, but a poster that was to make Frankie McPhee a legend. This poster, was a poster advertising the fact that the wrestling was to be held in the Caird Hall right here in the city centre. It said that all the big names would be appearing on the night. Not that it made any difference to Frankie, he couldn't read, but the poster had a drawing of two men wrestling and pictures of the faces of the wrestlers who were due to appear. That was enough for Frankie, he knew that the poster had something to do with wrestling, so he grabbed hold of a young boy who just happened to be passing, and made him read out what the poster said over a few times till he had all the details committed to memory, the day, the time, the price of a ticket, and when and where to get them.

Despite being bone idle all his life, and allergic to any time of day before 12 noon, Frankie was standing outside the ticket office at 5 o clock in the morning, four hours before it opened. Not that he had got up before 5 to be there, he just never went to his bed in the first place. It wasn't that he was scared of sleeping in, he was just so excited he couldn't sleep anyway.

This was partially due to Sticky Tam. He had planted in Frankie's head the idea that there were thousands of people wanting to go, and he might not get a ticket if he didn't go early to get a place in the queue, even then he might have to queue all day, so he better take something to eat and drink. So, Frankie had went along for his ticket at 5 o clock armed with a couple of pies and a bottle of Pineappleade.

Of course, he was the only one there at that time, and remained the only one right up until the office opened at 9 o clock. He mentioned to the woman behind the counter that he thought there would be more people waiting, but she just said she didn't know why, the organisers had only sent a couple of hundred tickets and didn't expect to even sell them, after all she said, it would be on the TV too. Frankie was a bit baffled by this, how could it be on the TV too, the wrestling on the TV was on a Saturday afternoon, and this was taking place on a Tuesday night, was the wrestling getting moved to Tuesday night on the TV? he asked. That would be great, he could watch it in the pub, he told her.

The night of the wrestling at the hall arrived, and again Frankie was first there, in order to get a good seat he had told the Usher at the door. The Usher explained to him that he had a seat number on his ticket, and that he had to find that seat and use it, not just sit anywhere he wanted, where did he think he was, at the Regal or something, be trying to buy a Butterkist and a Kiora next. Frankie just told him to shut his face and show him where the seat was.

Eventually, Frankie got settled in his seat and sat back to have a good gawk at the surroundings. He had paid the five shillings in order to get himself a ringside seat right in the middle of the row. Despite being the only member of the audience to so far turn up, the place was actually quite busy. The TV people were all busy making last minute tests of their equipment, the ring and ropes were being tested, and Kent Walton himself was sitting at the timekeepers table right in front of the ring. The hall eventually started to fill up however, and soon Frankie found himself sitting on his own. The people who had bought tickets for the seats either side and behind him soon started to wonder what that awful smell was and realising it was Frankie, moved away to find other seats, not at all happy at paying out for ringside seats and having to sit in unoccupied seats at the back, but thinking it was still better than having to put up with the stink from Frankie.

At 7 o clock the wrestling got under way. The first two bouts were between generally unknown wrestlers and were pretty well forgettable. The third bout was between two wrestlers who were quite well known and their appearance was intended as a warm up and taster for the real stuff after the interval. This third bout ended with some Hungarian Gorilla beating a Red Indian by two pinfalls to one submission. After the interval, there were to be two bouts and a tag match between wrestlers who had become household names owing to the wrestling now being on TV every week. These included some big huge fat bloke who always came in dressed in a kilt playing the bagpipes, and a dodgy looking Zulu who specialised in something called the Double Boston Crab, whatever that was.

The interval was to last half an hour, only so the organisers could sell as much stuff as possible, usually pies and tea, at the refreshments stalls. But tonight there was also to be an added attraction, a wrestler who looked like something you would normally throw nuts at in Edinburgh Zoo appeared in the ring. The MC, a little man dressed in a Tuxedo, then announced that any member of the audience who could last one three minute round with the wrestler would win a fiver. Frankie, who by now had nobody sitting within five seats of him, was sitting in his seat draining the last remnants out of a bottle of Pineappleade. A fiver! Before the MC could repeat the offer, Frankie was up on his feet and climbing under the ropes into the ring, like wrestlers when they got chucked out the ring. The man in the Tuxedo announced that they had a challenger as Frankie took his jacket off ready for the fray. After asking Frankie his name which was announced, the Referee motioned for the wrestler and Frankie to come into the centre of the ring to tell them the rules and whatever else Referees tell wrestlers. After a few seconds, the Referee and the Wrestler's noses began to twitch, and their faces take on a look of disgust. The wrestler realised the smell was coming from Frankie, so when he returned to his corner he started to climb out of the ring, at the same time telling the MC that he wasn't wrestling with that, just to give him the bloody fiver

II

One thing that was totally unique to the Rokie, was **Weelee Wags.** At least as far as I knew they were unique to the Rokie, because I certainly hadn't heard of them anywhere else. Just exactly what a Weelee Wag was, was open to discussion. From what I could gather, what with my Gran's and other descriptions, they were small, ranging from six inches to a foot in height, were very scary, had big pointy ears and teeth, wore a long pointed hat, and ranged in colour from white through every shade of grey to black. Seemingly, they were everywhere: under beds, behind wardrobes, up lums, down drains, in bins, in dark corners and long grass, in fact everywhere. They were the kind of thing generally used by mothers to get disobedient children into line. When they wouldn't come home at night, wouldn't stay in bed, wouldn't wash, or any other thing, the cry was that the ***Weelee Wags will get you*** Seemingly, if the Weelee Wags did get you, you would never be seen again, where you went or what they did to you was never explained, but that was it.

The Weelee Wags weren't the only scary things used to keep children in line in the Rokie however. There was also: **''The Hairy Hand''**. The Hairy Hand belonged to, or rather, **had** belonged to, Dan Doogan. How it had left Dan and was now going round scaring children is a bit of a tale, and one well worth telling.

One day, a few years or so back, Dan was making Hooch in a disused washhouse round the back of one of the empty tenements. The still was boiling and hissing away merrily, and Dan was sitting back having a fag waiting on the first drops of liquor to come through. He reached out to make an adjustment to something or other when suddenly without warning, the still blew up. The force of the explosion blew out the washhouse door and window and half the roof went up and came down again. The only reason that the place didn't burst into flames was due to the water in the still which went everywhere. Dan was also thrown back against the wall and it was a miracle he survived.

Within seconds of the still going up, Dan had recovered enough to get up and run out the now open door. He stopped a few yards away and surveyed the scene. There was still steam rising from the wrecked washhouse, and there was barley mash, water and glass everywhere. He looked down at himself, he was soaking wet, covered in barley, his head and face were scalded and his specs had disappeared. It was only when Dan tried to reach into his jacket pocket for his spare specs that he realised something else was missing. His left hand just wouldn't go in his pocket, and something didn't feel right. He held up what he thought was his hand, but all he could see was just a stump still dripping blood where his left hand had been. It was then that it all started to sink in. The shock of the explosion had put everything on hold, and now it was catching up fast. The stump started to throb with pain, and the scalds on his face and head started to burn.

Dan then realised that the bang must have been heard for miles around and hand or no hand, he better get the hell out of it, as somebody once said. He whipped off his jacket and shirt, put his jacket back on and wrapped his shirt round the stump. Dan then took off over a wall at the side of the washhouse and scarpered.

By sticking to the back alleys and Lanes, Dan arrived at the infirmary half an hour later. He refused to tell anyone what had happened, even the Boabees, who the infirmary staff had called in. However, once the report of an explosion in what was suspected to be an illicit still started to filter in, it didn't take them long to put two and two together.

Throughout the whole thing, Dan just stayed schtoom, and the Boabees eventually just dropped the whole matter, but not before giving Dan a serious warning on the dangers of illicit whisky making, never mind the legalities, and what he would get if he was ever caught at it, blah, blah, blah. They were also a bit hacked that the chief Boabee had insisted that a search be made for the missing hand, cant have a human hand just lying about, he had said. And so Slaberee Alec and a couple of others were sent to rake through the remains of the washhouse for Dan's hand. They never found it, and to this day its eventual fate has never been known.

The hairy hand keeps watch on bad laddies

A few days after the explosion, there were various sightings reported to the Boabees by callers. A black dog had been seen in Foundry Lane carrying a hand in its mouth, while another had been seen burying what looked like a hand round the back of Halley's. Now there was a thought, said the chief Boabee, what if a dog had got hold of it? So Alec was sent to check through the local dogs shite and ask the owners if their dog had brought home anything unusual lately. Not as simple a task as might be thought given the amount of dogs and dogs shite lying about the Rokie. Well, the word soon got round about Alec's investigation. Before long their were other sightings of the hand reported to the Boabees: The hand was being used to display watches and rings in the Pawn shop window, picking up fag ends in Foundry Lane, handing out leaflets for a sale in Markies, and playing the piano in Harry Bradley's. The chief Boabee soon got the message and the search was called off.

Dan's hand was never ever found, and its whereabouts to this day are a mystery. It did become a byword in the Rokie though. Along with the Weelee Wags, it was in constant use as a flegger of bairns. Mothers throughout the Rokie could be heard telling misbehaving bairns ***the hairy hand will get you.***

The hairy hand was also constantly being blamed when anything went missing. Bobs and half crowns missing off mantelpieces were blamed on the hand, as were fags missing out of packets and milk missing off doorsteps. Best of all though, was when Mary Thomson went home late one night minus her drawers and said it must have been the hairy hand.

Dan eventually got fitted with an artificial hand though. But for some reason he just couldn't seem to keep hold of them. The first one was made of some kind of metal over which he wore a black leather glove. That one managed to get run over by a tram one night when Dan fell in front of it drunk. There then followed a succession of hands made of various materials, all of which managed to get lost or destroyed in some manner or other. Like the time we went on a day out to the zoo and were all standing in front of a cage of monkeys. Dan reached out to give some nuts to one of the monkeys and it grabbed his hand and it came off. Dan got one of the keepers to try and get it back, but no matter what he did, the monkey just wouldn't give the hand back. Then Dan found that one of his customers, a retired carpenter, was into wood carving. He got the old boy to make him up a bundle of hands which he kept in an old tea chest. This way, he reckoned he had enough hands to last him the rest of his life. Unfortunately for Dan though, that wouldn't be for very long.

III

Every Sunday morning, starting at eleven, a sort of religious service would take place in the swing park on Blackscroft. The swing park was ideal for this purpose, basically because it was the only open space in the area. It was a large concrete square about seventy feet by seventy feet, with just two rows of swings, so left plenty of room. It did have railings and a gate, but the gate was never shut, and the lock was long broken.

At this service, along with a few prayers, the usual fire and brimstone sermon promising eternal damnation for those who indulged in the demon drink, fornication and the like, there was the usual singing, with the music provided by a band consisting of a Trombone and a Flugelhorn. The song sheets for the service, which were all hand written, were handed out by a couple of old wifeys who looked older than the bible, and probably were. Usually, a couple of dozen folk would turn out for the service, some of them regular attendees, and some who just happened to be passing and had bugger all else to do. The service usually lasted till about twelve or so, then, led by the band and a pair of devotees carrying a banner proclaiming that judgement was nigh or whatever, all would march around the three streets of the Rokie and back to the swings.

So, what was it all about? Basically, the whole shebang was run by a man named Cluny, and the term "man" is used here in its loosest form. Cluny lived just outside the Rokie in a house on the Ferry Road left to him by his mummy. He had no job, and lived in the house on money which was also left to him by his mummy. This financial independence meant that he was able to concentrate all his efforts on being a full time nosy bastard and bible thumper, something he did with great enthusiasm. To most folk in the Rokie, he was just considered to be a slimy little creep.

Cluny wasn't just a slimy little creep because of his nosiness and attitude though, he also looked for all the world like a slimy little creep. It wasn't all that unusual for folk new to the Rokie, or those visiting, to ask who that slimy little creep was the first time they saw him. Cluny wasn't that small really, but his hunched shoulders gave him the appearance of being shorter than he actually was. This wasn't helped either due to Cluny always wearing a long tan trench coat. He had also went bald on top at a young age, and combined with his big dark rimmed glasses and his habit of staring, it wasn't surprising that he got called what he did.

The story went, well, according to the locals, that because of the first world war, Cluny's mum and dad had met and married late, when both were well into their thirties. Seemingly, his dad was a big shot in one of the factories, and had made quite a bit of money. Not long after Cluny was born, his dad died as a result of wounds inflicted during the first world war, leaving his wife a bit of money, and Cluny to bring up on her own. According to those who knew, or at least said they knew, Cluny was the typical spoilt little shite, always wanting and getting his own way at home. Problem was of course, he was also one of those who thought this applied to the rest of the world, which in turn led to him getting more than the average belts in the face and dooings than other boys his age. I suppose this would explain his fear and hatred of boys.

Cluny, like a lot of boys, also started going to the BB as soon as he was old enough. For some reason he was never the spoilt little shite he was anywhere else, but unlike most boys who left the BB in their early teens, or when they found out that church attendance was a compulsory part of membership, Cluny stayed on till he was 18, then after as a leader. This probably had something to do with the fact that, along with his mum, he had already been a regular church goer since he was very young.

It seemingly all went wrong for Cluny when, in his thirties, he was thrown out of the BB. What the reasons for this were, like all the other stories that went round the Rokie, were basically just what folk said. Truth was, nobody really knew, or, at least, nobody said, or probably even cared.

Cluny had responded to this by not only leaving the BB and the church, but had also set up his own church and BB, the Boys Battalion. This had all started off ok, he had rented the old Kirky in Foundry Lane on Friday nights for the BB, and on Sunday for the sermons and Sunday school. Neither lasted very long however, as most laddies preferred the real BB. Those that did go to Cluny's new set up soon got fed up of the amount of bible thumping that attendance entailed. Eventually, he got the message and both the Boys Battalion and the Sunday school came to an end.

Cluny wasn't one to give up on his religious crusade though, he just took to other means. This was when he started preaching from the swing park on Sunday mornings. Cluny had hung a big banner from the railings that proclaimed various sorts of damnation for those who indulged in the demon drink, fornication, adultery, in fact, everything and anything. At first there was only himself and a couple of old wifeys. He would ring a big handbell to attract attention, and when a few people had turned up he would start the sermon. This would consist of a welcome to all his brethren, meaning those who had bothered to turn up. Then a hymn would be sung, usually one of those sombre ones with a lot of Jehovahs and the like in it. Then Cluny would read from the bible, always the old testament like Obidiah, or do and donts, mainly donts, out of Leviticus. Then another hymn, with him leading the singing at the top of his voice and cajoling others to join in. Then there would be the main part of the sermon, and this was where Cluny came into his own.

Ye who live among the clefts of the rocks

Within a few weeks he had maybe a half dozen or so devotees and a couple of musicians. Where he had dug them up, and especially a

Flugelhorn player from, was anybody's guess. Mind you, both of them looked like they were a few notes short of a tune.

So, there it was, every Sunday, come rain or shine, Cluny and his disciples would be there giving it laldy. At least it used to be every Sunday, till a certain TV event on Saturday afternoons changed it all.

IV

Graveyards, or boneyards, as we called them.

A few hundred yards along the ferry road, there was an old, disused and overgrown graveyard that hadn't been used for god knows how many years. The place was surrounded by high, crumbling, stone walls that kept the meagre light from the street lamps out, making it very dark inside, even on moonlit nights. At the entrance to the graveyard, there was a set of rusty iron gates The gate hinges had come away from the pillars, leaving the gates sagging in the middle, and so adding to the yard's sense of ancientness and disuse. These stone pillars holding the gates at the entrance, had solemn grave looking faces carved into them letting the passer-by know that this was a real creepy, eerie old place.

In one corner of the graveyard, there was a willow tree with long overhanging branches which covered some of the graves, and given the usual length of the grass, it was obvious the place wasn't tended very often. In the Autumn, the willow would shed its leaves and make the trunks look like huge arms coming out of the ground, with the branches looking like long tendrills and claws reaching down to the ground. This made the place look like something out of an Edgar Allen Poe story, especially on dark winters nights.

There was a real mixture of Gravestones in the Yard. As well as the inscriptions, there were urns, gargoyles, angels, crosses, some with masonic symbols and even some with skulls and crossbones and the like, which gives an idea of how old they were. Judging by the inscriptions, it was obviously a family place and all the names on the stones appeared to have some connection or other. Whoever the family were, they had obviously been well off as the stones were mainly marble, not many folk would have been able to afford that, especially in those days. Being marble, a lot of the stones were still in good condition and still readable. The oldest was dated 1760, but there was one just inside the gate that appeared to be quite recent, at least compared to the rest. For some reason, the stone on this grave was lying flat and was propped up a couple of feet of the ground. The Gravestone was very big and covered the whole grave, which gives an idea of the size of it.

For obvious reasons, this graveyard had been a bit of an attraction for the local bairns, especially on dark nights. Games of dare were often played, and stories of ghosts and white ladies were not uncommon. Any bairn new to the area would be taken right into the middle of the graveyard under the pretext that it was a usual place to go, then suddenly find themselves all alone as the others would run away. Most in the area had at one time or other went home in tears after being frightened half to death. But, there were others games that got played in the graveyard, and not just by bairns.

V

Not long after we took up Cossack dancing, my Gran took up football.

So, here we all are, the entire family, sitting watching our new TV. My uncle John had sent money, telling my Gran and Granddad to buy a TV set. It was Sunday night and we were watching Sunday Night at the London Palladium. One of the acts on the show was a group of Cossack Dancers, although whether they were Cossacks was debatable. Real Cossacks or not, we were transfixed by them. As soon as the show was over, we just had to give it a try. We soon found out it wasn't as easy as it looked, and we found ourselves falling about all over the place. Then it happened, as my older cousin, Billy, leapt in to the air with his legs wide apart trying to touch his toes. He came clattering down and cracked his head off the hearth. The blood came streaming down his face, and it was another trip to Maryfield. When the doctor asked what had happened, my Granddad's reply to the incredulous doctor was ***Cossack dancing.***

As usual, I was playing out in the street one night with the crowd, kick the can or something. It was one of these clear, still, very cold nights that nipped your ears and froze the snotters under you nose into a number eleven. I must have been caught or been out or something, as I was sitting on the kerb on my own when I heard the noise coming from way down the other end of the road. It was a sort of clumping sound, that kept repeating, sort of like the sound of a carthorse walking slowly on the cobbled street. I looked down the street, and could see a figure in the distance who appeared to be walking in time to the sounds, but it was dark and the gas lamps weren't much help, and whoever it was, they were still some distance away, so I couldn't make out who it was.

I decided that the mystery of the horse impersonator was more important than kick the can and started to walk towards the maker of the sound. As I got closer, I recognized the general shape and demeanour of the figure as my Gran. I then realised that it was in fact the usual time she came home from her job as an office cleaner at the sawmill where my Granddad worked. I walked towards her, and as I got closer, I saw where the clumping sound was coming from. She was wearing her usual coat, woolly hat, scarf and gloves, but on her feet she was wearing a huge pair of either football or rugby boots. They were the old type of boots that covered the ankles and had six big cork studs nailed into the soles, hence the clumping sound like a carthorse. As I approached her, I opened my mouth to ask her what was going on, and instantly got told that if I said a word I was dead meat. Knowing that she could knock out Benny Lynch with one wallop, I kept quiet.

Icy dub 1-Gran 0

After the initial shock of seeing her with the boots on, I followed her as she clumped her way up the stairs to the house. This was solely because my nose was bothering me as to why she was wearing the boots, and nothing else. My two great-aunties had also heard the noise coming up the close where it had been amplified to deafening proportions, and came out to find out what was going on. This is where my thirst for knowledge regarding the boots was quenched.

It was quite a simple explanation really. She had gone down to her work as a cleaner at the sawmill offices at half six as usual, and had taken the route she always used through the harbor gates and over the swing bridge to get to the sawmill entrance. But, as she stepped down off the swing bridge, what she didn't see or realise, was that there was a huge six inch deep dub frozen over and with a light covering of snow over it. As the rest of the ground was covered in snow, she just didn't see it and waded in with both feet, literally. Her initial reaction was to jump back onto the bridge, but as the cold water penetrated her shoes, she just decided to run for it. It took about half a dozen or so steps before she came out of the dub and was able to inspect the damage. Her shoes and socks were soaked through to the skin and her feet were beginning to freeze, so she just ran for the warmth and safety of the offices.

Once in the warmth of the offices, Gran got her soaking, frozen shoes and socks off, wrung them out and put them on top of the furnace in the boiler room to dry them out. She then set about cleaning up the offices in her bare feet. When she was finished an hour and a half later, she went into the boiler room to get her socks and shoes. The socks were dry enough, though a bit singed, but her shoes had completely shrivelled up with the heat from the furnace, and now wouldn't fit on to the feet of a five year old. She tried stretching them, bending them and forcing them on to her feet, but it was no use, they were ruined. She sat for a few minutes trying to think of what she could do to get home. There were phones in the office, but they were no use as nobody she knew had a phone. She could try walking home in her socks, but with the light covering of snow she never knew what she might stand in, glass, stones, or even worse. There were around twenty odd people worked in the offices, and there was all sorts of stuff lying around under desks, on top of cabinets and in the various cupboards. So, she decided to have a look round to see if there was anything she could use to get home. She found tennis racquets, balls, football shirts, towels, swimming trunks, cycle clips, golf balls, and, a pair of size 10 leather football boots with cork studs. Without a second thought, she sat down and pulled them on over her woollen socks, laced them up, tied them, and left the offices to walk home.

So, this was the tale she was now relating to my two great-aunties about how she came to be doing an impersonation of a Clydesdale horse pulling a coal cart. When they had finished having a good laugh about it all, Gran set off up the stairs to the house, and I followed, dying to see what my Granddad would make of it all. I ran ahead of her up the stairs, I wasn't going to miss seeing Granddads reaction to this one. I went into the house, and as usual he was sitting by the fire reading the racing results in the evening paper. I went over and stood across from him to get a good look when Gran came in. Seconds later, the clumping sound became louder as she came first in the front door into the lobby, and then through the door into the living room. When she was in the living room, Granddad lowered his paper, looked her up and down and asked her what the score was.

VI

Just after Tommy Dow fell in the washhouse boiler, Daft Tam had a scary experience.

Tommy Dow was at school with my cousin wee Dode. He lived with his mum up on Princes Street, and would sometimes come down to play with us in the Hutty. One day, we were having a game of cowsirs, when it started to pelt of rain. Our usual drill when this happened was to go into the washhouse round our backies or to the boaly. When we got there, we found that the washy was open, and that someone had fired up the boiler, so the place was really warm. Whoever it was had finished their washing and left the water in the big bowl that sat over the fire. The fire was still burning a wee bit, so the water was still very, very hot. The usual with this, was that the person who had used the washy, would use the old water to scrub the Close and stairs with. We had a sit about in the washy, and as usual before long we started pusying about. Tommy got up on top of the boiler and starts jumping around. Next thing, he slips and goes into the water up to his knees. At first, he just reacts by jumping out of the water and back down on to the floor. Then the pain hits him and he starts screaming. He pulled his socks down and his legs are bright red and has blisters starting to form. He can hardly walk, so we help him and take him back to his house. When we get there, his mum comes to the door after we knock. What happened next was the stuff of history. Tommy's mum let out a shreik, grabs him and starts shouting about what he had been up to now, then battered him.

One Saturday, Daft Tam had been drinking in Harry Bradley's from 11 o clock opening till half past two closing. Rather than hang about till the pubs opened again at five, he had decided to walk to Broughty Ferry a few miles away, just for a change. He reckoned that by the time he got there, the pubs would be just opening again. While drinking in one of the pubs, he had got in with a crowd who were going back to one of their houses for a party. Tam had talked the barman into filling a few empty beer bottles, and went off with the crowd. He left the party at around one o clock and started out to stagger the three or so miles home.

At god knows what time in the morning, Tam had been passing the old graveyard out along Ferry Road, when he felt the need of a piss. So, simple enough, he went into the graveyard for one. The graveyard was pitch dark and Tam fumbled and stumbled his way about looking for a place to do his business. After all, he said later, it was a graveyard, you cant just piss anywhere. After he had eventually found a suitable place and emptied out what seemed about half a gallon of what had once been good beer, he couldn't remember where the gate was. He staggered around in the dark trying to get his bearings, banging into trees and gravestones, falling over and fumbling for the gate, when he suddenly felt the ground giving way under his feet, and before he knew it, he was up to his waist in earth. Tam had tried to lift himself up out of the hole he had fell into, but found he was just getting more stuck as the earth collapsed round him. After struggling to get out of the hole for what seemed an age, Tam fell forward and leant his head on his crossed arms, exhausted, and eventually must have zonked out.

It was the middle of May however, and a couple of hours later it was light enough to see and the birds had started twittering. Tam woke up, wondered what the hell was going on and where he was. As he came round from his drunken sleep, he remembered the events of the night before and realised where he was, buried up to his waist in a hole in a graveyard. He struggled to get himself upright again, and looking around, found he hadn't in fact fell in a hole, but had fell into the grave of somebody called Joseph Duncan. Tam then did probably what any man would do in the same situation, and gave out a harsh, loud ***FUCKS SAKE!*** He then pulled out his tobacco and papers from his jacket pocket and rolled himself a fag. After smoking the rolly up, Tam decided he had better get himself out of the grave and get home, he was tired, thirsty and bursting for another piss.

Tam started to move his feet and legs around to get them loosened up. He could feel something hard and crunchy under his boots, and after a minute realised it was probably the bones of the grave's resident. Tam planted his hands on the more solid ground at the sides of the grave and started to push himself up. His legs started to move up, but after just a couple of inches he felt something grab at his left leg. The more he tried to lift, the more it held on to him. This threw Tam into a panic. What if it was the body? All sorts of horrors went through his head, and all he could see was himself being pulled down into the grave to be confronted by Boris Karloff or Lon Chaney. With a superhuman effort, Tam got his backside on to the ground at the graveside, got his hands on either side and pushed as hard as he could while shouting a stream of oaths. Suddenly, something gave way and his legs came up out of the grave. He dragged himself a few feet away and again collapsed in exhaustion.

After a few minutes, Tam got his breath back and stood up to have a look at himself. His good breeks were covered in earth and felt quite damp, while his boots were obviously full of earth and god knows what else. He gave himself a brush down with his hands, took of his boots, and holding them upside down gave them a belt or two on the gravestone to shake the muck out of them. He then sat down again at the graveside and put them back on. Once his boots were back on, Tam stood up, and looked down into the grave of the long dead Joseph Duncan. He felt the cool air on his leg and reached down to find that his breeks were torn where they had caught on to something in the grave. He again looked down into the grave and said accusingly ***Mi gaid breeks Yi ald cunt.*** Tam then turned and walked out of the graveyard and headed home.

Once he got home, Tam had a wash then went to his bed for a sleep. When he got up later that day, he made himself something to eat and had his usual only meal of the day. After his meal, he inspected his once good breeks, and found that the turn-ups were full of muck, and a couple of worms, and as well as being torn, they were ingrained with earth and grass stains. Tam realised that they were ruined and he would have to nip down to Paddys market and get another pair. Luckily it was Sunday, so the market would be open. He put on his work dungarees, which, like most men, were his only other pair of breeks. He cleaned up his boots as best he could, put them on and headed out of the house. On his way out of the Close, Tam thought he had better dump his now ruined good breeks in the bin, what with all them worms and the like. Coming out the Close after a visit to the bins, Tam realised it was Sunday, and so no pubs open. He thought to himself that after going to the market, he would jump on a bus out to the sticks and find a hotel where he could get a few pints. And who knows, might even meet up with one of them choochter lasses.

VII

The day after my Gran started giving fighting lessons, I developed a fear of midgets.

It all came about after my wee brother Davy came home from school with a pudden lip and a torn sark. I hadn't seen what happened, but seemingly he had had a set to with a laddie in an older class. I told Gran that I would batter the boy the next day, but she wasn't having it. She said he had to stick up for himself, and she would show him how. What a sight this was, Gran in the middle of the floor with her fists up, and Davy in front of her copying what she said. She told him to put his fists up like he was going to throw a punch, then when the other boy is watching his fists, kick him in the shin, when he drops his guard due to the pain in his shin, stick the head on him. Granddad meanwhile, who is sitting reading his paper, drops the paper and shakes his head in resignation. It worked though, Davy had his last ever fight the next day.

Next day, I woke up with a dose of the skitters. My Gran kept me home from the school and I spent most of the morning in the outside toilet reading old comics. By dinner time, it had started to ease off and as I managed to eat my dinner, Gran gave me a note for school and told me to go back for the afternoon. The note just said to excuse me for being off, nothing about the morning only, so to hell with that.

I decided to go for a wander down by the docks and then along to the foreshore. As long as I kept out of sight of any Boabees, especially Slaberee Alec, I would have an afternoon of freedom. Not as attractive a proposition as I thought though. It just wasn't the same on my own, and after about an hour, I was fed up. I thought about going to my Granddads work and asking for a bob for the show, but I knew that no matter what tall tale I gave him, eventually it would get back to Gran, and I'd be for it. Nothing for it, but to make the best of it.

A while later I found myself on a bit of waste ground between the docks and the foreshore. There were tents and caravans all over the place, and it was a hive of activity with all sorts going on. It seemed that a Circus had set up home for a spell, and I went over to see what was what. I went into a big tent and found it was full of strange looking animals, some in cages and others tied to posts. I had a wander round, and the thing that stuck out most, was the unbelievable stink. Then I noticed why, there was shite everywhere. A man covered in tattoos asked what I was up to, and I asked him what had made a particular pile of shite. He replied that it was a Camel, and another pile next to it was a Llama, and yet another was a Hippo. He continued to point out other types and before long I knew the difference between the shite of an Elephant, a Lion, a Llama, a Chimp, a Sea Lion and a variety of other wild animals. The tattooed man then said I better be on my way, so I said thanks to him for telling me about all the different types of shite. He just said that if I ever got offered a job as an explorer or a big game hunter, it might come in handy.

The midget and the honest laddie

Anyway, I left the tent and had a wander round. After a while, I heard a voice beckoning what I took to be me. I turned and looked in the direction of the voice, and there, standing in a caravan doorway, was the smallest midget I've ever seen. He beckoned me to go toward him, and when I did, he walked along a plank of wood that ran from the door of the caravan and on to a chair. He had very short dark hair, and was wearing a dirty, grimy vest that had been white at some time in the distant past, and a baggy pair of jeans with god knows how many turnups. On his feet, he was wearing a pair tackety boots that were obviously umpteen sizes to big for him.

When I got in front of him standing on this chair, I was just a little shorter than him, so he was able to look down at me, which was probably the whole object. He looked me up and down and sideways so intensely, I thought he was going to sniff my arse next. In a voice like Tommy Trinder, he said *you look lak a good led*, and I assured him I was. Next thing, he reaches into his pocket and pulls out a ten bob note, hands it to me and says if I go to the shop and get him twenty fags and a newspaper, I can keep a tanner to myself.

I made a mental note of my Granddads warning about smoking stunting the growth, this boy must have been smoking about 200 a day since he was about three. I took the note, and half an hour later I'm sitting in the Regal watching Samson and Delilah and eating a Mivvi, a tub, peanuts, Butterkist, a Bounty, a Choc Ice, Maltesers, an Aero, drinking a Kiora.............

VIII

It was about the time I got a kick in the arse for tearing my good breeks, that an Irish Navvy met Daft Margaret.

One Sunday afternoon, my Gran washed and polished me till I was gleaming. I had my only decent set of clothes on, which were only for very special occasions. It turned out we were going to the christening of one of my umpteen cousins in the local Kirk. Once I had eaten my fill of cake and peeces back at the house, I went with the gang out to the backies. While we were deciding what to do, old Mrs Hickey came out and asked me to put up a rope for her on the pulashee. She was only on the first Pletty, so it wasn't much of a climb. However, after putting the rope through and dropping it, I slipped and fell the 15 feet or so to the ground. When I landed, I felt a sudden pain in my hand, and noticed I had torn my trousers. My Granddad, hearing me howl, and the others all shouting, came running down the stairs. He checked me over, and said it looked like I had broken my finger, so up to Maryfield again. As I started to walk away, he shouted *is that yir gaid breeks yiv toarn* and gave me an almighty kick in the arse.

The houses in the tenement just past the swing park had windows round the side that overlooked the swing park. Two floors up, one of these houses was occupied by a woman known as daft Margaret. Although called Daft, Margaret wasn't actually the slightest bit daft, she was just as mad as a hatter. There were countless tales about what had happened to her: being jilted, losing a child, fell on her head, you name it. Her madness showed in various ways, such as her habit of throwing objects at any source of noise she considered annoying, and she had a deadly aim. The rag man doing his rounds with his bugle always took care when blowing it near her house ever since a lump of coal bounced off his head a couple of years earlier. Quite a few after hours opera singers had been known to turn up at the Infirmary after being clocked with various items, such as tins of soup, bars of soap, pots, pans and the like. Cluny and his band would especially take care to keep the music level down.

One day, something happened that was to have a profound effect on the Rokie. Daft Margaret went too far and they had to put her away. Not that the recipient of her madness made a complaint though, he didn't, he was just too embarrassed to let the Boabees take any action against her.

It happened a few days after some Irish Navvys started digging away at the road on Blackscroft, sorting the sewers or some other shite that Navvys do. Anyway, Margaret came along shoving an old pram. In the pram was her weekly washing, and she was heading up to the public washhouse a few streets away. One of the Navvys said something, and of course the rest joined in causing Margaret to let off her usual stream of oaths, curses and general abuse. A couple of hours later, she was heading back home from the washhouse with her now clean washing in the pram. The Navvys, seeing her coming, started to give it the nudging each other and here she comes muttering. Margaret heard this and started her ranting again. One of the Navvys then dumped a shovel full of dirty, stinking, soaking wet earth into the pram on top of her clean washing. Give Margaret her due, she never reacted, just paused, then on she went. Less than two minutes later, she came back. This time however, she was holding a poker which she cracked the offending Navvy round the head with. The Navvy grabbed his head, gave out a loud ***OYAH!*** then fell poleaxed into the pile of earth he had been digging.

According to Slaberee Alec, who went to investigate after hearing about the incident, the Navvys head was in a right mess and needed a whole tin of Elastoplast. Well, that was it, although no complaint was made, Slabberee Alec told his Sergeant about the episode, who told his Inspector, who told his chief Inspector, etc, till it reached the chief Boabee himself. By what mysterious, officious means, nobody knew, but one day the green van with square wheels turned up and Margaret was taken away. The Rokie was never to be the same again.

IX

In the Rokie there was no shortage of wildlife. In particular, there was not a shortage of cats. They were everywhere, big ones, small ones, fat, scrawny, striped, patchy. They could be friendly, timid, fierce, and came in a range of colours, black, white, ginger, and believe it or not, pink, red, blue, yellow, green and just about every other colour imaginable. This was due to the fact that there was a dye works in Foundry Lane. So it wasn't unusual to be walking along the road and seeing a pink cat wandering about. It just depended on what colour the cat had fell into.

Although the residents of the Rokie were used to these kind of sights, it could still cause a bit of consternation to visitors. Like the time a couple of German sailors found themselves in the Rokie and had got blootered in Harry Bradley's. The two sailors had left Harry's at half past two closing time, walked along the main road, and stopped to have a seat in the Library gardens. It had been a hot day, and there were a lot of cats about, lying in the sun soaking it up as only cats seem to be able to do. The sailors just couldn't believe their eyes at the sight of a bright blue moggy lying sprawled on the hot stone slabs of the Library gardens. They just stood and jabbered away in German, pointing at the cat. Then when a large bright pink cat came right up to one of them and started rubbing itself up against his leg, the two of them went into near hysterics. It can only be assumed that the topic of their conversations for some time to come would be about the strength of the beer in Harry's.

Most nights, lying in bed, the sound of distant, and not so distant, screeching and squalling could be heard as the local cats fought out the disputes that I suppose cats had disputes about. That, and the racket made by tabby cats on heat looking for a good seeing to, could, on some nights, be deafening. The fights in particular sounded like they could be quite vicious, and there were some well known contenders among the Rokie cats, especially at heavyweight. For instance there was Ludwig, a large, but a bit fat moggy that belonged to and old man who lived on Blackscroft. All day it would sit out on the window sill on the second floor and just sleep. How it never turned over in its sleep and fell of the sill was a mystery. The cat got the name Ludwig because its owner was a big Beethoven fan, and all day the strains of the 9th or 5th would come wafting out the open window where the cat would lie sleeping. But come the night, and Ludwig was often seen out on the prowl, getting up to whatever cats get up to when their prowling about at night. He was a fighter of some renown and had often been seen chasing some other cat that he'd just beat the shite out of. But he had also been seen getting chased after taking a beating of some other tougher moggy.

One of these tougher ones, was Ogenthorpe, the king of Halley's mill. Its not hard to describe a cat like Ogenthorpe, he looked for all the world like a brigand. Half of one ear was missing, while the other was in shreds. He only had one eye, half a tail, and had umpteen patches where the fur had been ripped off. But by far, his most frightening feature was his teeth. How it came about could only have been a freak of nature, but he had two top teeth that protruded down over his chin making him look for all the world like a sabre toothed tiger.

Ogenthorpe got his name from an old boy who he had previously lived with. The old boy was also called Ogenthorpe and had worked in Halley's for some time. Just before he retired, he had found what he thought was an abandoned kitten in one of the warehouses. He had taken the kitten home and it lived with him there till he retired a couple of months later. When the kitten got older, it decided to go back to live in Halley's. Ogenthorpe kept going back for it and taking it home again, but the cat just kept going back. A few months later, the old boy died. Not long after, the cat was seen hanging about the door of the house where he had lived in Foundry Lane. The new occupants of the house put food out for the cat, but wouldn't let it in. Of course, as food had been put out, the cat would come back to the house occasionally, but in general stayed at Halley's. As nobody knew what the cats name was, the fact that it had belonged to the old boy, Ogenthorpe seemed as good a name as any, and the name stuck.

Also on the heavyweight contenders list was another one of Halley's cats called Tonto. Tonto was actually ginger in colour, but after he turned up covered in bright red dye one time, somebody or other had christened him Tonto. As if the red dye wasn't enough, he must have been getting wired into a pigeon or something, as there was a feather stuck to his head with blood.

Then there was the king of all the Rokie cats, the one and only Shug the Thug. Shug had started out as my Granddad's cat when he had brought him home as a kitten from his work at the sawmills. About a year later, Shug moved into Harry Bradley's. He followed my Granddad there one night and planted himself in front of the fire. At closing time, he just refused to leave, and just like some bothersome drunk had to be thrown out. As usual, he went away out on the prowl that night. Shug's usual behaviour was to go on the prowl all night, then next morning he'd be waiting on the doorstep to get in. Once in, he would get fed then sleep all day before going out an the prowl at night again. He wasn't waiting at the door the next morning when my Granddad went to let him in. When Granddad went for a pint to Harry Bradley's that night, there was Shug, lying in front of the fire. According to Harry, Shug had been waiting on the door step when he turned up at the pub at nine o clock that morning.

Shug was also ginger, pretty big, but not as big as say, Ogenthorpe or Tonto. But what he lacked in size, he more that made up for in bravery and out and out visciousness. Shug really was an out and out thug. There wasn't a cat in the Rokie that he hadn't sorted out at one time or another. It wasn't just that he would beat up the local cats, if new folk moved in to the Rokie, or a cat from another area came in looking for god knows what, then Shug would have to go round and pay it a visit, just to let it know what and who was what.

Shug's nickname didn't just come from his carry on with other cats though, he could, and generally was, just as vicious with people and other animals. Many a mutt in the Rokie had come to grief just because it thought it could chase Shug. And many's the person who thought they would pet the cute cat sitting by the fire in Harry Bradley's. The only person who was allowed near Shug was my Granddad. Shug had obviously not forgotten his early days sitting on my Granddad's knee, and the titbits of food he used to get. Cats weren't the only animal life in the Rokie though.

X

Another thing there was no shortage of in the Rokie, was snakes.

Frankie McPhee got the fright of his life when he got up one day at the crack of dinnertime, went through to the front room, opened the curtains and a huge Anaconda was staring right at him, fangs bared with its jaws open and venom dripping off its long forked tongue. So much of a fright that after initially being frozen to the spot, he turned and ran through to the back room slamming the door shut behind him and standing with his back against it keeping it secure. A couple of minutes later, after Frankie stopped shaking and regained his senses, he opened the door very slightly and looked nervously with one eye through the crack and saw the snake was still there in the same position. As he finally woke up fully, he realised what had happened while he slept through the morning. When he told Sticky Tam about this later in the day, Tam reassured him that it was ok, Anacondas weren't venomous, they wrap around you and crush you to death before eating you. Frankie thanked him for putting his mind at rest, it was a big reassurance to know that.

    Why was Frankie so scared though? after all there were snakes all over the place in the Rokie: big ones, small ones, red, blue, yellow, green, black, white, multi-coloured, striped, venomous, constrictors, they were everywhere: on stairs, walls, drain pipes, doors and windows. Victor Mature was holding a Cobra by the tail and beating the shit out of the Philistines with it on a Samson an Delilah poster, while on another poster, a toothy woman was brushing her teeth with what looked like a very pissed off Python. The best however, was in the phone box at the top of the November stairway where a coiled up Rattlesnake appeared to be having a snooze on the floor. It had been there for over a week, and so far nobody had went in to use the phone.

So, where were they all coming from? The snakes were in fact the handiwork of one, Luca Savic, a lad who lived in the Rokie. He had drawn the snakes all over the Rokie with crayons. Although still just a Laddie, Luca was a very adept artist, and particularly very good at copying pictures precisely. Why snakes? Well, it was a long story.

In 1947, after the end of the war, not the war to end all wars, but the one they had after it, Janos and Eszter Savic took their four year old son, Luca, and walked the 878 miles from the town of Dorog in Hungary to the port of Rotterdam in Holland. A journey that took them near seven months through war torn Europe to cover. At Rotterdam, they stowed away on a boat bound for the city, and arrived at the docks a couple of days later. Why here? Janos's uncle, Tibor, a circus strongman, had come to the city some years before with a travelling circus, met a local lass, and had ended up staying. His uncle's letters had spoke fondly of the city, and for some time Janos had been thinking of joining him. The war decided it for him.

Janos's uncle Tibor had done well for himself in the city, he had put his talents to good use and got a job with the gas board digging holes. He had also gotten himself a house in the Rokie, in one of the tenements beside the paper shop on Blackscroft. When Janos arrived, Tibor had no problem with helping him out, despite only having a two roomed flat. Tibor had also helped Janos to get a job beside him with the Gassy, also digging holes.

Janos and Eszter had to stay with Tibor and his wife near three years before they eventually got a house of their own. When they did move, it was only a few yards away to a house above Robertson's grocers shop. By this time they were a family of four, as wee Gorgi had been born the year before.

Luca and Gorgi were well known in the Rokie, Luca for his artistic talents, and Gorgi because he was such a lovely, likeable wee laddie. What endeared him to folks was his big permanent grin and friendliness to everybody. Him and Luca were inseparable, despite Luca being ten years older. Often, they would come along to the Hutty and play with us, and although Luca was older than us, it was good to have a big laddie around in case of any marauding gangs of laddies from other areas, like the Watson streeters, who we had a particular enmity with.

XI

School in the 50s was another place for some off the wall events and characters, and the school I went to was no exception.

If there's one day that sticks in my head, and probably most people's head, about schooldays, its the first day back after the seven weekies. It was so bad, that even the night before was a non event cos of the thought of it. I tried staying awake as long as

I could, trying to put off as long as possible, the inevitable. But, as usual, there was just no escaping.

In my case, it was waking up to the mid August sun streaming through the window. Normally, I would have jumped out of bed, into my clothes and out the door, no washing, no breakfast, just out and up to something. Not today though, I got up and went through to the front room. My cousins, Wee Dode and Ronnie, and my half brother Davy were there, sitting at the table, while wee Tam was asleep on the bed settee. My mother and step dad, and my auntie and uncle worked, so before leaving the house the bairns were all brought to my Grans to get ready for school. After a lot of mumping, moaning and near a couple of fights breaking out, we all got ready and left the house for school.

We got to within sight of the school, and found to our dismay that it hadn't been burnt down, the war hadn't restarted and it had been hit by a bomb, the sky was clear so no chance of a lightning strike, so on and in we went. I met up with my classmates and went through the usual of what we had done during the holidays, which in most cases was what we done any other time. Then the teacher came out blowing a whistle, the bell sounded and we all lined up.

Once in the lines, we noticed that our class had moved up. This was due to a class having left for secondary before the holidays. All the classes marched into the school and again lined up, this time in the hall. After the usual welcome back from the Haidee, followed by a hymn and the usual lengthy prayer, we were told which classroom we were to go to. For us, this was room 7, and a teacher we had never heard of called Miss Pearson.

After assembly, we went into room 7, and found an ancient old wifey sitting at the teachers desk. She told us all to sit anywhere, which we did after the usual scramble for the desks at the back. Once settled, the old wifey told us she was Miss Pearson, and was our new teacher. We all looked round at each other, cos even as young as we were, we could tell she was well past her sell by date. My Gran was 60, but didn't look as old as Miss Pearson. Her face was well wrinkled, she had gray hair held up in a bun, but it wasn't till she stood up we realised just how ancient she must have been. It took some effort, with her hands on the desk she pushed herself up to a standing position. She was quite stooped, her shoulders hung down and she moved with what seemed an aching, creaking effort.

A few years later, Miss Pearson's death notice appeared in the local paper, giving her age when she died. It worked out that Miss Pearson was 78 years old when we had her. At the time, the council was building a lot of new houses in the peripheral estates around the city. This meant a lot of new schools, but also a problem in that there was still the same amount of teachers for double the amount of schools. So, in their wisdom, the council dragged a whole load of ex teachers out of retirement, including Miss Pearson. They had also got some student teachers who were supposed to be supervised to take some of the classes, but that's another story.

Miss Pearson, despite her great age, turned out to be much the same as any other teacher we had. There were a couple of things that stand out in my memory of her though.

The first was regarding the fact that she could hardly walk. She had two sticks and it was obvious that walking was a real effort to her. She would turn up at the school every morning in a taxi, which would pick her up in the afternoon again. When she got to the school, she would take an age to climb the four flights of stairs to the floor where our class was. Once there, that was her there for the day. As the staff room was up another four flights of stairs, one of the other teachers would take her a cup of tea at the intervals, while the dinner wifeys had to take something up for her at dinnertime. What she did for the lavee was beyond us, and obviously the topic of much disgusting speculation. One late morning, she obviously couldn't wait any longer. She told us to sit and read a poem, and that she would ask us questions about it later. She then left the room. A couple of minutes later, we could see her climbing the stairs to the top floor. My pal Dode summed it up in a oner when he said that she must be needing a shite. Nuf said!

Another great memory of Miss Pearson was reading lessons. Most of us in the class, like most folk in the city, spoke a mixture of plain English, words unique to the local accent, and plain English words spoken in the local accent. For some reason, us using the local accent used to drive Miss Pearson mad. She would rant on at us for ages if we slipped into using it. One day, I was asked to stand and read a passage from some corny book that was a standard text for eight year olds. It was about some family sitting down to their tea, and I had to read out: ***Mother picks up the pot and pours out the tea.*** Fair enough, but to me, in the local accent, the word pours is pronounced **poors,** which I said. This is the way I had always heard it, and so what do I know that's different. She went berserk when I said **poors.** You'd have thought I had just set the school on fire or murdered the Haidee. She made me say ***Mother picks up the pot and "POURS" out the tea*** about ten times, with a final warning to *"**NOW REMEMBER THAT".***

It was the same with Pete Chalmers one time. He was sitting at a desk right in front of Miss Pearsons desk. He turned to Jimmy Broon who was sitting beside him and said in all innocence: ***wonder whats fir the dennir the day?*** She picked up a book and threw it at him, hitting him on the arm. Next thing, he was on the receiving end of a tirade about ***DINNER NOT DENNIR AND ITS FOR NOT FIR A FIR IS A TREE!!!*** We all sat in astonishment while we got a ten minute rant about using proper words in English and that we would never get on speaking our own accent as nobody but ourselves would understand and how we would never understand wonderful things like Dickens or Shakespeare. Rant! Rant! Rave! Rave! Shakespeare? And here's us thinking Shakespeare was a chip shop down the road, and how we always understood the owner Vince.

The best however was a boy called Eck. Same as me and Pete, Eck was told to stand and read a passage from some book. This book was about a boy going on a sailing trip with his uncle, not exactly an everyday event to us. Eck stood up and started to read: ***Tom was going on a trip on his uncle's yacht.*** Only thing was, Eck pronounced **yacht** in the same way Germans say **nacht,** and the same way we said **ach** in our local accent. Those of us who knew he had got it wrong instantly looked at Miss Pearson to see her reaction. Sitting at her desk, her head fell forward on to her hands which were on the desk, she then then started to shout ***Yacht! Yacht! Yacht! Yacht!*** over and over about twenty times finishing with ***Yaaaaaaaaaaaacht! You stupid boy!*** Just like me, Eck had to say it over and over again till she was satisfied. She then wrote **YACHT** on the blackboard in foot high letters, and about a dozen times during that day, she would ask him how it was pronounced. Eck told us at playime he really though that was how it was said, he'd never seen the word before, and why wasn't it spelt **y-o-t.**

Another thing that stands out was when she read stories to us. To do this, she would sit on her desk with her feet on the chair, facing us. Under normal circumstances, and with most other teachers, there would'nt be a problem with this. But, and there was one almighty but, with her feet up on the chair and her legs wide open we could all see right up her skirt. What a sight that was. In complete oblivion as she read us a story, we were given a full view of her bloomers down to just above her knees and stockings to just below her knees.

It's a sight that is forever engraved on my memory, unfortunately. A mate of mine, who went to a catholic school, once told me that the boys at his school were given a talk on sex by a priest. According to this priest, if you had thoughts of a sexual nature, and started to feel your knob stirring, just lie on your side and say a little prayer and it would go away. Obviously, there were no Miss Pearsons at his school. To this day, I'm not sure the whole thing wasn't a Calvinist plot.

Although this display was quite traumatic and happened a few times while we had Miss Pearson, it was nothing compared to what did happen and led to her abruptly leaving the school.

One day, just before the Christmas holidays, after we had had Miss Pearson for about 5 months, we all trooped back into the class after dinner/dennir. It was obvious she couldn't be bothered with us as she was even more crabbit than usual. She just kept telling us to sit down and be quiet. When we had finally settled down, we were told to open our arithmetic books and jotters and do all the sums on pages 10 and 11. Now, it was cold outside being winter, but the room was stifling and we had just had our dinner. So sitting here in the quiet doing boring sums meant us feeling a bit sleepy. And obviously we weren't the only ones. After about 10 minutes of this, a sudden grunt sound filled the room. We looked up and saw that Miss Pearson had zonked out at her desk.

Miss Pearson zonks out in class

For the next couple of minutes, we all sat and looked at each other sniggering. Then a boy at the back got up on his desk and did a little dance. This was the cue, and next thing we were all at it. Paper planes were flying, some girls were throwing a tennis ball back and forward, a couple of boys were jumping from desk to desk the length and breadth of the room, all in total silence. Pete Chalmers, who sat at the front, got up on his desk, turned round, bent over and wiggled his arse right at her.

All of a sudden there was a sound of the door opening. We all looked in the direction of the sound, and there was the Haidee. We all froze. He looked round the room at us in our various silent activities, then there was another grunt as Miss Pearson let out another snore. In total silence, the Haidee opened the door fully, then motioned for us to leave the room. We all trooped out into the hall, the Haidee Closed the door and told us all to go out to the playground, keep quiet and wait for him to come out. About quarter of an hour later, he came in to the playground and told us to gather round him. We were told to stay in the playground, but to stay quiet till after the interval. The girls then went back to their skipping and we continued our game of walk the plank.

At the interval, the rest of the school came out, and various activities went on as normal. After the interval, we were told to return to our class, which was empty, no Miss Pearson. A couple of minutes later, the Haiddee came in, set us some sums to do, then sat with us for the last hour of the day. At the end of that school day, the Haidee told us to come back to the same room, but that we would have a new teacher. And that was the last we saw of Miss Pearson.

XII

Louie the Next had inherited the tailors business from his old man, who was also a tailor, and had taught Louie his trade. The business was mainly alterations and repairs, and most of the custom came from Boabees, bus and train drivers and the like. He also got quite a bit of work from running up made to measure suits from people who couldn't get off the peg clothes and couldn't afford to go to the big established firms in the city centre. This was generally people of unusual size, like very fat, very tall or very short. Sometimes it was people who had come by a bit of cloth and fancied a suit made of it, or sometimes Louie would come by a roll of cloth himself and would run up a few for off the peg sales. Any leftover cloth from his made to measure customers would also be run up into suits, trousers and waistcoats for off the peg too. The stuff was cheap by the big store standards, and folk weren't usually that fussy about size or whether or not stuff even matched. Some old boys in particular would buy a jacket, trousers and waistcoat all in completely different colours and patterns.

Sticky Tam had once asked Louie how many different parts there was to a three piece suit. Without thinking, Louie had walked right into that one, and said sometimes as much as thirty different parts, depending on the style. There was the sleeves, lapels, collar, pockets, pocket flaps and various other parts. Okay, said Tam, and asked Louie to make him a thirty piece suit, with every part made from a different colour and pattern of cloth. Louie had said it would probably take a long time to make, but Tam said no problem, he wasn't in any hurry. Seemingly the suit took eighteen months to finally get together. Tam had it hanging in his wardrobe and said he was just waiting on the right occasion to wear it.

Louie the Next had come by his nickname in a simple manner. Basically, one night in Harry Bradley's many years before when Louie was a young man and his old man was still alive, he had, as usual, been sitting having a drink and a read of the paper. It turned out, at round this time, some daft King or other of somewhere or other, Wullie the Ninth or Eck the Tenth or the like, had dropped dead. There was seemingly a bit of a stushy about who was to succeed him. Somebody had asked where all this "The Somethings" came from? Why was it always The First or The Second or whatever number? Louie had said that his dad was called Louie as well, so when he died, he would be the next in line, what would he be called? Louie the Next, said Sticky Tam. The name had stuck ever since.

At the time that I remember him, Louie the Next was probably in his late 50s or early 60s. He was a dapper wee man whose philosophy was that nobody would want to use the services of a tailor who looked like a sack of of shite tied up with string, so anytime Louie was seen out and about, he was always wearing a neatly pressed suit, which seemed to change every few months, courtesy of leftover cloth. He would also always wear a shirt and tie with the suit, brown suede shoes and a fedora hat.

He was a wee man, Louie, round about five feet two and slightly built. His wiry hair, once dark, was greying, and when it was seen on the very rare occasions when he took off his hat, it was, along with his mouser, always neatly trimmed. Louie done alright by his tailoring. At least he made enough for a man of simple tastes like himself. For obvious reasons, he didn't have to bother with money for clothes, his home was part of the business, so any money for rent, heating and the like was paid out of the takings. His only real outlay was for food, for which Louie had very little appetite. Besides, Louie had had a problem with his stomach for umpteen years which meant he could only eat the simplest of foods, which didn't cost much. He had been told by a doctor years before to cut out fried food and drink, both of which Louie loved. He would give up one or the other, but not both. The fried food lost, and so Louie's main diet consisted of nips of Hundred Pipers and bottles of Mackeson.

Louie was also a very quiet and sombre man. Anytime anybody met with him, he would always acknowledge the meeting with a little nod of the head and occasionally a hmm or a hi, that was it. If somebody stopped, or when he stopped, it was usually because there was some news or gossip on the go. This quietness and sombre nature was probably a result of the long hours Louie spent in his own company working away at his Tailors business. Passing by the pawn shop and looking up, there was nearly always a light on in his workshop no matter what the time of day or night.

As far as anybody knew, Louie had always been a bachelor. Seemingly he had only ever had one romantic interlude in his life, when he was in his thirties, and had met a woman at the Palais or something. She had been married before and had a couple of kids, and, it seemed Louie had been quite taken with her, and she with him. But, after a while, she had tried to change him. She had wanted him to stop going to Harry Bradley's, start working more regular hours and what have you. Well, Louie by this time had become set in his ways, and was a bit too fond of his few nips and Mackeson in Harry's, and so he called it all off. Seemingly she married a bus conductor and emigrated to Australia. Louie was fond of his nips and Mackeson okay. Every day, round about half twelve, he would go down to Harry Bradley's and have three or four nips of 100 Pipers and a couple of bottles of Mackeson. It was the same at night, from around seven to closing time, he would sit and drink, read the paper, and occasionally join in a game of bones. That and a couple of packs of Woodbines every day and all was well in his world.

XIII

Round about the time Obvious Joe got a new pair of underpants, Louie the Next had the first of a series of really weird dreams.

Louie had been sitting in Harry Bradley's one day and was just starting on his usual dinner of three nips of 100 pipers and a bottle of Mackeson, and, as usual, he was also doing the crossword in the day's paper. Also, as usual, bang on twelve, Obvious Joe came in and as Louie was the only person in the bar, he planted himself at Louie's table. Louie sat, not looking, and waited for Obvious Joe to say something obvious, like, ***doing the crossword are you***. But, it appeared nothing obvious was forthcoming and so Louie waited. Five minutes passed and Louie started to get irked, he wanted to be left in peace and just wanted Joe to state the obvious and bugger off. Joe was up to something, if Obvious Joe was not being obvious, something was coming, and Louie knew he was about to walk straight into it. He looked up, and Joe was just sitting there, leaning back in the chair with his arms folded over his big belly and a smug look on his face. Then it arrived full force, and Joe blurted out *I got a new pair of underpants the day*.

Later that day, Louie sat in his workshop listening to an American salesman who was trying to sell him some shirts. It turns out that the American government had put the shirt industry on full pelt production during the war making army and navy shirts. At the end of the war, they were left with millions of them and so decided to sell them off. This salesman's firm had bought a load and were going round trying to sell them off in wholesale lots. The salesman had seen Louie's sign at the Close entrance and thought he would give him a try. Louie looked at the sample shirt, it was light blue, and made of that new stuff, nylon, and according to the yank, it only took a quick dip in water to get it clean, and hung up, it would dry in a few minutes. Would certainly suit folk round here, he thought, they don't have much in the way of washing facilities. The salesman offered him a carload for a fiver, so at a couple of bob each he wouldn't have to sell many to be in profit. He didn't even have to pay the fiver till a month after he got the shirts, couldn't lose really, so he said OK.

Anyway, that night in Harry Bradley's, Louie was on round his fourth nip when he mentioned that day's transaction to Sticky Tam who was sitting playing bones at the next table. Tam asked Louie to verify that the salesman was in fact an American. After receiving Louie's confirmation to this question, he then asked him if he knew what a carload was in America, and that it was in fact a railway carriage. Louie's silence confirmed that he didn't know, but concealed the fact that he had silently shit himself. A railway carriage load, there would be thousands of them. What the fuck was he going to do with all those bloody shirts? Where would he keep them? It would take years to sell them all. Later that night, Louie went to bed with shirts and railway carriages lying heavily on his mind.

Next day, Louie answered a knock at the door to find a man in railway uniform asking where to put his delivery of shirts. Just bring them up here Louie replied, to which the man asked if he was kidding. Louie decided he better have a look and went to the window. His worst fears were confirmed, there in the street were five lorries, all piled high with light blue, nylon shirts. The drivers had another dozen or so men with them, and they all started to unload the lorries and carry the shirts upstairs to Louie's house. In they came to the living room carrying bundle after bundle of shirts, dumping them on the floor.

Louie went out to the street and found that the men were still only on the second of the lorries. The men were still unloading and carrying huge bundles of shirts into the Close which was near to full. A bit of a crowd had gathered to watch what seemed to be a bit of a carry on, while some of them were helping in the unloading and carrying. Louie sat down on the kerb, lit a fag and leant his head on his hand.

Half an hour later, one of the drivers came over to Louie and asked him to sign a bit of paper saying that he had received the shirts. Louie signed without even looking up, he never even noticed the men piling onto the lorries and driving away. Louie finished his fag, slowly stood up and turned round expecting the worst. Nothing could have prepared him for the sight he was about to see though. The shirts were piled high right along the pavement, while the Pawn shop, Harry Bradley's and the nood book shop had all disappeared behind a mass of blue nylon leaving only space for the doors. He went over to the Close and looked up, there was only a narrow passageway as the shirts were piled up to the ceiling on either wall. He went up the Close and found the stairs were the same. Louie pushed his way up the stairs between the piles of shirts and got to his door. He had to climb up onto the top of the piles and across the top to get into the house. When he got in, Louie crawled across the mass of blue in the lobby, into the workshop and over to the window. He looked out of the tiny gap at the top and could see that the back green was piled high with the shirts, and that the Washhouse roof had disappeared under them.

Louie needed time to think, he crawled over the shirts and through to the living room. He got to where his bed was buried under the blue mass of shirts, lay back, lit a fag and seeing that the ceiling was only about a foot away, shut his eyes. What the fuck was he going to do? He heard the sound of Halley's siren and wondered what it was going off for, it couldn't be that time, could it? He opened his eyes and the ceiling wasn't a foot away, but was a good six or seven feet away, where it should be. He rubbed his hands on the sheets and realised they were cotton, not nylon, and looking round he could see the shirts had vanished, it was just a dream.

.I dream of shirts

Louie lay for a few minutes to get the sleepiness out of his bones and head. He then got up out of the bed, stretched, farted, put the kettle on and went for a pee. Also, as was his usual, he then made a pot of very strong tea and put on the wireless. Louie then sat down and lit his first fag of the day awaiting the coughing fit that was sure to follow, which it did. Once the morning ritual of stretch, fart, kettle, pee, tea, wireless, fag and coughing fit was over, he settled down to sit and enjoy the fag and his first of around 5 or 6 cups of very strong tea. As always, Louie sat at the table side on, legs crossed with his head resting on one hand and with his elbow on the table. He was sitting there listening to the news programme that he listened to every morning. He was half way through the third cup of strong tea, when he remembered the shirts and said out loud ***Thank fuck that was just a dream.***

XIV

It really is a major disappointment, when on hearing some earth shattering news, you rush out to tell everybody, and they already know. So it was with the Lone Ranger. My Granddad had seen the notice in the local paper and read it out to me. I went tear arsing out of the house, down to the lane and went up to the gang and blurted it out. To my disappointment, and sudden anger, they already knew. I twisted about in frustration for a few seconds at this, but the topic of conversation was about going to see the Lone Ranger in person at the Greens Playhouse in a weeks time, so I quickly relaxed and joined in.

At the time of the Lone Ranger's appearance at the Greens, I was 9 years of age. At that age, play was usually taken up with games like Japs and British or Cowsirs. Most boys had toy guns, so the games took on an element of realism, well, for us anyway. As this was not long after the war, some boys also had stuff that their dads and uncles had brought back from their armed service. So a game of Japs and British could involve participants carrying bayonets, helmets and bits of uniform or packs. Problem for me was that my Granddad had been in the navy, so not much point in carrying about a 6 inch shell case, a bosuns pipe or wearing a sailors collar and a pair of navy dress shoes.

Cowsirs was our main game though. There were so many western shows on the TV and films at the cinema, that we didn't have a lack of inspiration for our games. I remember a new boy whose family had moved into a house on Blackscroft and who introduced himself as the Laredo Kid. There he stood, two holstered guns, a white cowboy hat, a tasseled waistcoat, khaki shorts, wellies and a number 11 snotter hanging under his nose. Randolph Scott had nothing to worry about.

Guns were also a big issue to us then. It just wasn't the same pointing a finger and shouting bang, and some manufacturer somewhere knew this and had cashed in big time. There was a huge range of toy firearms around in the shops, generally made of plastic or cheap metal. Nearly all could fire caps, and the makers also cashed in by introducing rolls of caps as well as individual ones. A couple of months before Christmas one year, I spotted a particular cowboy gun in a shop window on Princes Street. It was wonderful, it had a revolving chamber like a real cowboy gun which tilted out to one side. Once tilted, it had bullets that could be removed. When the bullets were taken out, a cap could be put in the chamber, the bullet put back and when the gun was fired, the barrel revolved to the next chamber, just like a real cowboy's gun. I had to have it. I noticed however, that it was about four times the price of the other cap guns. So, it would have to be a big occasion present like Christmas. It was a couple of months to Christmas, so plenty of time to drop a couple of hints in my Gran and Granddads direction. Anyway, the 5 or 6 thousand subtle hints *like* **have you seen that gun in Preston's window, the one that cost 15 and 6,** or ***imagine a toy gun costing 15 and 6*** must have worked, cos I woke up on Christmas morning at 4 o clock to find it in my stocking. One big problem though, no bloody caps. Neither were there any shops open. Later that day, along with 40 other boys who had got cowboy stuff for their Christmas, I took part in the re-enactment of the Gunfight at the OK Corral. But I was the only boy who did have a gun, but still had to shout bang.

It was with this gun that I went to see the personal appearance of the Lone Ranger at the Greens Playhouse. It turned out that there was to be a Lone Ranger look alike contest with prizes. On the day a whole load of 7-10 year old boys turned up in the most unlikely and bizarre get ups imaginable. For my own costume, I had pestered my gran into making a shirt and matching breeks, just like the Lone Ranger had. Only problem was, having a black and white TV, as did everbody else, she had no idea what colour they were. So, she gets an old pair of curtains and makes them out of the cloth. My outfit consisted of matching shirt and breeks, (grey with orange roses), a white hat, mask and wellies. Unbelievably, mine was actually one of the more sensible outfits, and I came 27th in the look alike contest. Not bad out of near 3000.

XV

It was near the time we got a season ticket to Maryfield casualty department, that some Tinks visited Harry Bradley's.

I suppose bairns fall out over the simplest and sometimes daftest things. Like me and wee Dode one day falling out over a nood book. We had found it on a bin raking expedition round the back of the bakers in Princes Street. We were actually looking for cakes when we found the book, called Health & Efficiency. After an hour or so in the Hutty going through the book, we started home. That's when we fell out. Dode had the book, and said he would hide it in the loabee behind the door, while I said I would take it and hide it in the boaly. As we were pulling at the book, I pushed him and he fell over. When he landed arse first, it was right on top of my uncle's tool bag. The bag had a file without a handle sticking out and this is what Dode landed on arse first. Problem was, the spike that a handle would be on had barbs on it for keeping the handle on. So, the file wouldn't come out. As my uncle was still at his work, it was up to Maryfield again for Granddad and wee Dode with a file hanging out his arse. That was the ninth time that year Granddad had been to Maryfield with one of us. The doctor, who obviously had a sense of humour, gave Granddad a piece of paper with **Season Ticket** written on it.

Saturday nights in Harry Bradley's were, like most pubs, the busiest night of the week. Unlike during the week, on Saturday night there was a mixed company with women being around half of those present. With Harry's being the only pub in the Rokie now, he had only recently relented to women in the bar. A few of the regulars who went out with their wives on Saturday, were talking about going somewhere else if they couldn't bring them in. This had led to a sort of sing song on Saturday nights that would start around eight o clock and go on till closing time. Despite there being a piano, the sing songs were usually conducted without a musical accompaniment as nobody could play it.

A couple of local characters, Mick Feeney, who had only recently moved to the Rokie, and a boy called Wullie Broon, fancied themselves as singers. Wullie in fact, fancied himself so much, he had started calling himself Johnny Athens, to give himself an air of showbiz. Mick declared himself Master of Ceremonies and would start the night with a couple of numbers, usually Frank Sinatra stuff, and would then introduce those who had put their names up. Those not willing to give a song were cajoled into an attempt by promises from Mick to join in, and threats of being given a **Hehburdeefleh.**

During one particular Saturday night sing song, a crowd of Tinks turned up, prompting Sticky Tam to ask Tinky McLairen if they were relatives of his. Half an hour or so later, Dan Doogan had just ended a particularly murderous rendition of I Will Take You Home Kathleen, which had brought tears to the eyes of a couple of those present. This had brought the comment, again from Sticky Tam, that the song hadn't been that bad. As soon as Dan had finished, one of the Tinks produced a melodeon which he started to play. Now Mick took his position as MC very seriously, and told the Tink to put up his name to give a tune and wait his turn. The Tink nodded and stopped playing. The next up for a song was an ancient old wifey called Maisy McNabb singing some shite called The Special Years. She only got through the first couple of verses before she was overcome by the emotion of it and started crying. This brought murmurings of sympathy, and offerings of grotty **hunkys** which she received with sobs and tear filled eyes, and of how it reminded her of her long dead Wullie. Mick asked everyone to give her a big hand, and before he got a chance to introduce the next act, the Tink with the melodeon started up again. Again Mick told him to stop and wait his turn, and again the Tink stopped. To cheer everyone up after the last singer, Mick then broke into a version of Sweet Sixteen which was greeted with a round of applause, except from my Granddad, as this was his song. Those who knew the song started to join in and shout encouragement for others to do the same, before long everyone had joined in. Even Harry, behind the bar, had joined in while drying glasses. Mick was up on his feet conducting the choir which was now swaying to the time of the song. The end of the song brought a great cheer and clapping, all of which Mick took to be for him and he gave bow after bow. Then, the melodeon started up again.

Mick again told the Tink to stop, only this time the Tink kept playing. Yet again, Mick told him to stop and wait his turn. One of the other Tinks then said that he had waited long enough, and told his mate to keep playing. What happened next was talked about for years after.

As the Tink kept playing, his mates all started to sing some song that only they knew the words to. Mick went over to where the Tink was sitting, grabbed the melodeon, stretched it out to its full length, raised it, and brought it crashing down on the Tinks head. Suddenly, everybody in the bar went silent and looked in the direction of the Tink. All that could be heard was the off key sound of the dying melodeon. The two wooden ends of the instrument hung either side of the Tinks head, and the concertina part in the middle had come right down to just above his eyes with the wires sticking out the top.

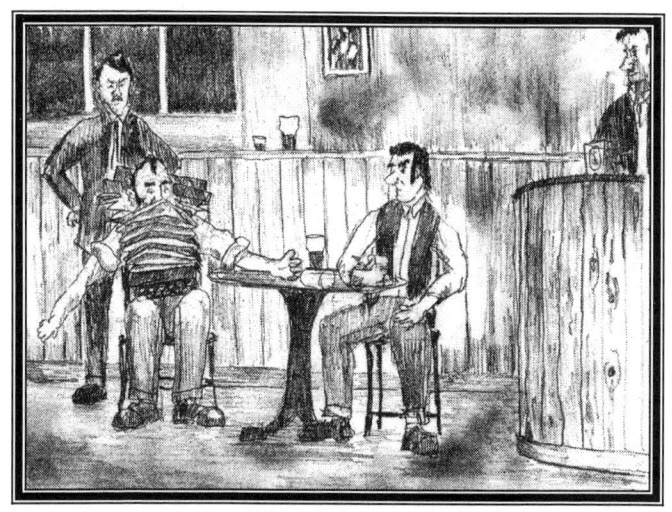

The dying melodeon

The Tink got up, and as he did, the melodeon gave off another couple of notes as the ends bounced up and down. As those present started to recover from the initial shock of what had happened, a huge roar of laughter broke out at the sight of the Tink with a melodeon stuck to his head. Even the Tinks mates were laughing. The Tink reached up and pulled the instrument off his head and examined it, dropped it on the floor and threw a punch at Mick, which he dodged like a boxing pro. The Tink then went to throw another, but before he had even drew his fist back he was entangled in the big muscular arms of Harry. Before he knew what was what, the Tink found himself out in the street. His mates, who had also thought the whole episode funny, suddenly started to lose their sense of humour at the sight of their mate being dragged out the door. Then, when Mick picked up the now wrecked melodeon, opened one half of the swing doors and chucked it out into the street after its owner, their mood changed altogether. One of them, nearest the door, called Mick a wee shite and went for him. Now Mick was quite wee, but unlike the Tink, he was only in his early thirties, was exceptionally fit with working on building sites, and when he was younger, had been a good amateur boxer with the chance of going pro. The Tink swung a punch, but before he knew it, Mick had landed him a classic triple combination: one to the stomach, one to the ribs, and to crown it all, a punch to the jaw that would have flattened an elephant. The Tink went down on to one knee, it had all happened so fast he didn't know what to hold, his ribs, guts or his probably broken jaw. Harry then directed a couple of the regulars to hold the swing doors open, grabbed the Tink, picked him up and dragged him too out into the street. One of the three remaining Tinks then grabbed a pint glass off the bar, he took aim and threw it at Mick. Mick saw the move and ducked, the glass flew across the room and smashed into the photo of Nelson hanging above the mantelpiece. On seeing this, Sticky Tam got up from his seat, barged across the bar and cracked the Tink one in the face. The Tink replied to this with a punch back to Tam's face, and this was the sign for a general melee.

Before anybody knew it, the place was like a scene from a cowboy film. There was fists flying, glasses being knocked over and smashed, teeth being either knocked out or taken out by those joining in, women screaming, and bodies flying through the swing doors. Harry went back behind the bar, locked the till, and came back round to join in again. The punch up lasted only a couple of minutes, and ended when the last of the Tinks had been put out.

The following week, a similar incident occurred involving a Teddy Boy and a Guitar, so Harry put a stop to the sing song nights, at least for the time being, they were just too dangerous.

XVI

One night, I got sent to Dora's chip shop up on Princes Street. When I got there, I was met with the sight of two obviously drunk men sitting on the pavement with their backs leaning against the wall. They were eating fish suppers out of the newspaper wrapping, which they were washing down with a bottle of Vimto. It was the two German sailors who had got such a fright at the site of the multi-coloured Rokie cats. Being so near to the docks, there was always a lot of sailors of all different nationalities wandering around. I had always been fascinated by the different languages, and liked to ask what was their word or phrase for whatever. So, I said hello to them, and they seemed amiable enough. I asked them where they came from and they replied Hamburg. I asked what was the German for chips, and one of them said, **Apfel fritte.** I then asked the usual stuff, like cowboy, which was just the same, then Boabee, which is **Polizist,** and was delighted to find that I lived in **Gück Tag Gasse.** After a few attempts I worked out that **Kreigsmarine Bleu Unterhosen** is Navy blue knickers. Then I had a sudden idea. I asked how to say **Eech Meech Hens Keech Toly Bum Fart** in German. Eech meech is an old Dundee children's saying, and is used for picking sides in a game. It took a while, but I eventually arrived at **Eisen Meisen Honsen Scheissen Kaken Popo Furtsen.** The Eisen Meisen is just there to rhyme with Scheissen.

XVII

Occasionally, apart from his fire and brimstone sermonising, Cluny would also rent the old day school on an odd night here and there. On these nights, the local bairns would be asked to come along to the school where there would be games and quizzes with prizes, but of course, still managing to squeeze in a bit of the usual bible thumping. On one of these nights, an incident occurred that was to eventually lead to some unforeseen and murky consequences.

As usual, after Cluny had spent a couple of nights going round the streets on his bike asking the local bairns to come along, a crowd of them turned up. On one particular night, we were all out playing in the street when we saw the other bairns heading for the hall, so decided to go and see what it was all about. Luca, who was with us, said he'd come too, and his wee brother Gorgi, who was only four, insisted that he get to go as well and so we took him along.

Part of the so called fun, was when bairns were asked to go up on the stage and sing a song, or recite a poem or whatever. Of course, this led to the usual Mary My Scots Bluebell, I Love a Lassie and the like. There was also poems such as: My Love is Like a Red Red Rose, or There was a young cricketer from Neath, while batting got hut in the teeth. I found myself sitting next to wee Gorgi, who sat listening intently to the poems for some reason or other. Then, he asks me what a poem is. I tried to explain that its when the words at the end rhyme, but I can tell he just doesn't get it, after all, he is only four. I recite the one about the cricketer from Neath and the word teeth, then another about the old man from Montrose who got bit in the nose, and suddenly his face lit up. Next thing I know, he has his hand up and Cluny points to him and asks him to go up on the stage.

So, up Gorgi goes on the stage and Cluny asks him what he's going to do. A poem, says Georgi with a big grin on his face. What happened next, was something so gob smacking that it should be up there with Homers Odessey. Gorgi just stood there and let it rip: ***Tarzan in the jungle, waiting on a bus, alang came a monkey and skelped him in the pus.*** The silence at this was deafening. Hear a pin drop? If a mouse had farted, it would have sounded like a Brass Band. To make it worse, Gorgi just stood there, waiting on his round of applause from the audience, and the sweetie that everybody else got. But nobody made a sound, and Cluny and his sidekicks just stood there like they'd just had the death sentence pronounced on them.

Even us rif raf who were always up for a laugh, just sat open mouthed in awe struck silence. Then the silence was broken by one of Cluny's old wifey helpers who told Gorgi that that was very good and here's a sweetie as she ushered him back to his seat.

After recovering from the shock, Cluny must have thought it would be good to have a change of tack, and asked an old wifey to start playing Jesus Wants Me For A Sunbeam on the piano. She started to play and then sing while Cluny urged us all to join in. Some did, while us riff raff, now recovered from the shock, started to sit and dig each other in the ribs and have a good laugh at Gorgi's recitation. A couple of minutes later, I happened to look up at Cluny and what I saw made me freeze momentarily. He was staring right at Luca. It was a cold stare, emotionless, no malice, no hatred, just nothing, a blank, unblinking stare, like I had seen on a snake in the zoo that time my uncle had took us.

Later that night, I realised what that stare had been about. Cluny obviously thought that Luca had put Gorgi up to the malarkey with the poem. Nobody knew it then, but that look had been of malice and hatred, and one that was to lead to murder, but whose.

XVIII

One day, for the first and only time in my life, I saw someone eating a roll on a roll.

On days when the weather was pleasant, the men from Halley's would come and sit out the back of the mill at dinnertime. If we were off the school, this was always an opportunity for us to make a couple of bob. Some of the men would ask us to nip down to the shops and get pies, sausage rolls, filled rolls, bottles of Pineappleade and the like.

Putting stuff on a roll was not unusual in these parts, or probably anywhere for that matter. A well known delicacy hereabouts was a pie on a roll. Most places that sold made up rolls would make you any combination your heart desired: mince; chips; chips and peas; peas on their own; mince and tatties; bacon and egg; bacon, egg and black pudding; the list is endless; down at Ruby's café, you could even get a deep fried roll. But a roll on a roll takes a bit of explaining, and it turns out it had something to do with nippy cheese and Tyree's well fired rolls.

One such dinnertime, when I was off the school for whatever reason, electing a new village idiot or something. I saw this old boy taking two rolls out of his piece box, he opened one roll out, put the other roll inside it and proceeded to eat the both of them. I waited a while, then overcome by curiosity, asked him why he had done it. Simple, he informed me, he liked to have two of Tyree's well fired rolls, and he also liked a thick slice of nippy cheese, which was a particularly strong Canadian Cheddar. I was still a bit bemused, so I asked him a series of questions which he answered without hesitation. Now, this is where the complicated bit comes in.

Why not have two rolls both with cheese?

No! he could only eat one thick slice of nippy cheese.
Why not one roll then?
He liked two rolls.
Why not have a thin slice of cheese on each of two rolls?
He liked a thick slice of nippy cheese, not a thin slice.
Why not one with a thick slice of cheese and one without?
He didn't like a roll without nippy cheese.
At this point, I tried to think of other permutations but realised that the only solution to this particular dilemma was in fact to put a thick slice of nippy cheese on one roll, put it on the other, thus creating a roll on a roll.
Nuf said?

XIX

As well as there being no shortage of cats or snakes in the Rokie, there was also no shortage of dogs, or **doags.**

Although dogs weren't seen around all that much in the area, the evidence that there were a lot of dogs was obvious, the amount of dog shite that seemed to be permanently lying about. The shite, although occasionally useful for the tricks we got up to, was a pain. This went especially on the occasion when you unknowingly stood on it in the dark and then trailed it home. It not only meant having to scrape it off your shoe, but also clean up whatever else it had got on to. I mind one time my Granddad had trailed some home, and was sitting with his feet up on the fireplace. It wasn't till my Gran came home and noticed not only the trail of shite across the floor, but also the fact that there was shite on the mantle piece and halfway up the wall. Most dogs around the Rokie appeared to be strays, not that they were homeless, just that they were allowed to roam around free. This could lead to some funny episodes.

One such episode was when my Gran put out a big pork roast on the doorstep to cool. It was Christmas day, and we were all sitting in my Grans house waiting on the dinner. All of the family who lived in the Close were there, eight adults and five bairns. They had all chipped in and bought an enormous pork joint, all the veg to go with it, and a massive trifle. About a half hour before we were to eat, Gran took the joint out of the oven. It was absolutely red hot, and just not ready for carving. Granddad had borrowed a knife from a local butcher for this, and had taken advice about letting the joint cool down. As it was roasting hot in the wee house with the oven having been on all day, my Gran decided to put the joint out on the doorstep. Half an hour later, she went back out to the door to retrieve the joint, and it wasn't there. After letting us know about this, we all went out to the Pletty. There was suggestions as to the whereabouts of the joint, like one of the neighbors had swiped it, or a huge seagull or pigeon was away with it. Then, looking down into the backies near the bins, I saw a dog that appeared to be up to something. When I mentioned this, my Granddad and uncle Dode went down to investigate. As they approached the mutt, it gave out a low growl. When they got Close to it, they could see that it was this dog that had knocked the joint and was now having a feast to itself. Grandad and uncle Dode then had a bit of a conflab, and came back up the stairs. When hearing that the potlicker did have the roast, my Gran told them to go and get it. Granddad's reply to this was quite simple ***Em no eating it eftir that potlicker's been slaberrin a ower it.*** So, Christmas dinner that year consisted of roast and mashed tatties, sprouts, carrots, peas, apple sauce, gravy and a **Fray Bentos pie.**

The most famous dog in the Rokie though, was Sputnik, the dog that belonged to Tinky McLairen. It wasn't anything that Sputnik did, it was Tinky's reaction to something that happened to Sputnik that made him well known. Sputnik got his name through Tinky getting mixed up with the name of the Russian dog, Laika, that was sent into space, and the spaceship that took her. Sputnik was a mid sized dog, and was obviously part collie. He had got the dog as a pup on a trip with Tam out to the country one time they were looking for wood. The farmer who had gave him the dog said it was too mixed up a breed, and wouldn't be any use on the farm, so he could take it. Tinky and Sputnik went more or less everywhere together. If Tinky went somewhere dogs weren't allowed, like the show, Sputnik would wait outside for him. One time, the two of them were in the Coaly after rabbits. While raking about in a clump of weeds, Sputnik suddenly gave out a yelp and came running back to Tinky. On having a look, Tinky could see that the dog had been bit by something. On looking in the weeds, he could see it had been a hedgehog. Whether or not it was the hedgehog bite, or Sputnik had got something else from it, a couple of weeks later, Sputniks hair started to fall out. Within a couple of months, he was totally bald. Having a bald dog didn't seem to put Tinky up or down, neither did it seem to bother Sputnik. This however was over the summer months. Round about the end of October, when the nights get earlier dark, and the air is a bit cooler, Sputnik started to show the signs of his hairless state. Tinky started to notice it too, and what he did about it was the stuff of legend. He bought Sputnik a coat. Not one of those doggie coats made of tartan, but an actual coat, in fact a duffle coat. The boy working in Menzies on Princes Street, could hardly believe his eyes, when after buying a child's dark blue duffel coat, the customer took it outside and put it on a dog. Not only that, but Tinky liked the coat so much, he bought one for himself. This was the sight that for some time was common in the Rokie, a man and his dog wearing matching duffel coats. If a stranger to the area saw them and asked why the dog was wearing the coat, Tinky would just reply ***Well, whut im i supposed ti dae, eez freezin.***

XX

Just after my Gran and Granddad went on a cruise, I took a trip back in time.

One morning, a letter appeared though the door. It was from my uncle John who was away at sea. Apart from the usual stuff about his adventures, there was a fiver and an invitation for my Gran and Granddad to join him for a couple of weeks. It turns out he has landed a job on a cruise ship on the Baltic, and it would be coming to the city to pick up fuel, supplies and passengers at the end of the month. He has also managed to wangle a cabin for Gran and Granddad on the ship, and they would be going to places like Hamburg and Helsinki. Gran wasn't all that keen, but Granddad was looking forward to his first trip on the high seas since he came out of Wavy Navy in 1950. I wasn't mentioned in the letter, and was a bit hacked that I wouldn't be going, but there was to be some news for me too.

One of my Mum's older sisters, my auntie Margaret, lived in the west end of the city. She was married to my uncle Johnny and had two bairns, my older cousins Colin, who was four years older than me, and Jane who was the same age as me. As it was the Dundee fortnight when Gran and Granddad were going to be away, my uncle Johnny would be on holiday too. My uncle had a motorbike and sidecar, and they were planning on going for a day here and there during the holidays. It was arranged that myself and one of my other older cousins, Stewart, would go and stay with them for the fortnight and go on the day trips as well.

Anyway! The Dundee fortnight duly arrived, and so did the monsoon season. For the entire two weeks, it just never stopped raining. My uncle Johnny had to spend his entire holiday pay on taking us to the show every day, sometimes twice a day. It was either that or being cooped up in a two roomed house with four bairns all day and night. Then, one day, he took us for a trip back in time.

After a look through what was on at the shows in the paper one day, it was decided we would go to see a rerun of The Vikings at the Peak. Uncle Johnny said that he wanted to leave early, as he wanted to drop in to see his Mother and Father, my cousins Gran and Granddad, who lived near the show. We got the bus over to Princes Street, then went up the long climb of Dens Brae and William Street. A good bit up William Street, we turned left into North George Street and went up a close a few doors along. After climbing what seemed to me about the height of the **La Hull**, we arrived in the attic. There was a small square landing with what I took to be the outside lavee, and to either side a long, very narrow lobby seemed to end at nothing. We went down one of the lobbys, and uncle Johnny chapped at one of two doors about halfway down that were facing each other. A voice from inside asked who it was, then on hearing uncle Johnny's reply, told us to come in.

Nothing could have prepared me for what I was to encounter inside the door. When we had all got inside, a voice asked uncle Johnny to put the light on, as even though it was only dinnertime, it was very dim in the room. When he pulled a box of matches out of his pocket and reached up, I realised that it was gas lighting, something I had heard older folk talking about. Once the room was lit up, I had a good look around. It was like being in a film of a Charles Dickens story. Where do you start describing a scene like this. We were in a room about 18 feet long by about 10 wide. The facing wall, which I took to be the outside wall, and actually the roof, sloped down to only about 3 feet high making the room seem smaller. In the middle of this wall, there was a space about 3 feet wide which had a recess. In this recess, there was a tiny window, sink and cooker. The window was so small, and being north facing, that hardly any light came in. At one end of the room, there was a fire surround made of dark wood, inside which sat a tiny cast iron fireplace. On either side of the fireplace there was an armchair, and on the wall next to the door, sat an ancient sideboard. At the other end of the room, there was a double bed lying across the room with one side up against the wall. It was one of those beds with high wooden ends, and the mattress was a good couple of feet off the floor. In this bed lay two people, one on the inside next to the wall, that I took to be the Gran, and the other on the outside who I took to be the Granddad. Next to Granddad's side of the bed was a cabinet. On the top of the cabinet was various items. There was a lamp, some candles and a saucer to put them in when lighted, a couple of pipes with various tins and pouches of tobacco, a big box of matches and a bottle of Abbots Choice whisky.

When the room was lit, it was still quite dim, probably due to the gas being kept down. The Gran, after a lot of effort, scrambled her way to the outside of the bed, put on a cardigan over her nightgown and headed for the recess to put the kettle on. We all managed to find a seat of some sort, with Colin and Jane being asked to sit on the edge of the bed beside the Granddad. He had sat up in bed by this time, and I could see he was in fact very old. Along with a pair of striped pyjamas, he had on a multi coloured tammy with a tassel on top. He asked them about how things were and how they were doing at school and what have you. We all then went and sat at a folding table that had been set up in front of the fireplace. God knows where it all come from, but along with a pot of tea, there was a big plateful of mixed tea bread and jars of various jams.

After we had our fill of tea bread and tea, the Granddad asked my uncle to go to the window. He then gave instructions on how to take it out of the casing. Uncle Johnny asked what was wrong with the window, was it loose or something. The Granddad then told him to take it out of the casing and bring it over to the bed, which he did. When the window was on the bed, the Granddad produced a bit of scrunched up newspaper from a bedside cabinet drawer, then asked Colin to get him a bottle of vinegar from the press, which Colin went and got. We all sat transfixed as he then used the paper and vinegar to clean the window. Even uncle Johnny looked amazed by this. When the window was cleaned, he then asked uncle Johnny to put the window back in the casing. When it was back, I could see a distinct change in the amount of light there was now in the room.

I really thought I had seen it all, but what happened next really put the lid on it. The Granddad asked Colin to put the used cups and plates in the enamel basin that was sitting in the sink. When this was done, he then said to fill it with hot water and again to bring it over to the bed. Once the basin was sitting on the bed, Granddad then produced a bar of coal tar soap and a **cloot** from the cabinet drawer, and proceeded to wash the dishes. Jane was asked to go over with a dish towel and dry them and put them back in the press. But incredibly, this comedy show still wasn't over. Granddad then brought out a shaving brush and a razor and used the water to have a shave.

When I finally got back home after Gran and Granddads cruise, I told my Granddad all about uncle Johnny's dad. The story I got, was that on his retirement at age 65 in 1948, the old boy had went home, gave the pension and bank books to the Gran, then went to his bed and had been there ever since. That meant at the time I was there, he had been in bed for 11 years, and was to remain there for another 6, making it a world record 17 years in his bed. I didn't dare ask at the time, but eventually found that the toilet arrangements were an Edgar Allen under the bed for pissing, and bottles of Kaolin to constipate him, so he only went for a shite once a once a month with the aid of a few tins of prunes.

That wasn't the end of the saga though, far from it. 4 years later, the Gran died and the Granddad went to live with uncle Johnny and auntie Margaret. He initially stayed in bed when he went to stay with them, but when they moved to a house in the schemes, the bedrooms were upstairs. My auntie Margaret decided she just wasn't putting up with serving him in bed anymore, and eventually after a lot of mumping and moaning, he got up. It took a while, but he then had a new lease of life. He started looking after the garden, going for walks and day trips with the family, and even got in a fight. This was when one of the elderly neighbours, who was a real crabbit old git, had been giving the bairns a hard time. My cousin Colin told me that one day they had been out with the tennis racquets when the old boy had come out blowing a whistle and telling them to go away. My uncle Johnny had originally went along to have words with him, and had come back raging about what he would do if he was an older man, or the old boy was younger. Granddad, standing at the door puffing on a pipe of Bogey Roll, had asked what was wrong. My uncle told him, then went away in the house with steam coming out his ears. A couple of minutes later, Colin said he looked along where the sound of raised voices was coming from, and saw Granddad with his fists up having a go at the old moaner. He had went along and claimed him. It worked though, Colin said, no more whistles or mumping from him. Anyway, after a couple of years the Granddad had went and got pissed one day, and there was a bust up at home over it. He left and went into an old folks home where he met a woman 10 years his junior. They wanted to have a room together, but the home wouldn't let them as they weren't married. So out of sheer devilment, they did just exactly that. He was 87, and she was a sprightly 77. My cousins Colin and Jane were the witnesses, and they got their photo on the front page of the Tele.

Once I got home, I also got the story of the cruise. Not it all though, Granddad and Gran were quite reluctant to talk too much about it. It was when my uncle John came home that I got a better idea of what it was about. Seemingly, my uncle had been glad to see the back of Granddad, and regretted ever getting him on the cruise in the first place. According to my uncle, Granddad had been so taken with being back at sea, he had taken to resuming his old rank of Killick, Leading Seaman, and had started ordering everybody around. **That's not how you tie a rope, that's not how you steer a ship, whats that doing there, move it.** It wasn't till near the end of the cruise, when he near got a belt in the pus from a Hamburg docker, that he settled down. So, all in all, what with a Baltic cruise and a trip back in time, it was an eventful two weeks.

XXI

Individual sports requiring great strength like weightlifting and wrestling seem to be a thing with Hungarians. Janos was no exception and was a great wrestler. On Sundays, he would take on all comers for half a crown over three-three minute rounds in the swing park on Blackscroft. He had managed to get hold of a big Gymn mat from somewhere, and had laid it out in the park. Uncle Tibor, also a one time wrestler, would referee the matches which would always attract a bit of a crowd. Men from all over the place would turn up each week to have a go, not just for the half crown either. Wrestling had become a bit of a favourite the last while due to its coverage on the TV on Saturday afternoons. A lot of men, especially young men, fancied themselves at the game and saw this as an opportunity. Some saw it just as a good laugh and something to break the boredom of a no pub Sunday. It wasn't all about Janos either. Janos was a big man, unlike many in these parts, and it wasn't always easy to find a match for him. So, the smaller men would be matched up with each other.

It all started off simply enough, but eventually the regular wrestlers started bringing their mates along to act as seconds. They'd bring bottles and buckets for water, and towels and sponges. Janos himself wore a pair of proper wrestling boots and pants, the long tight ones with straps that crossed and went up over the shoulders. Others just stripped to the waist and wrestled in their breeks and boots. Tattoos however, were the general order of the day and all the wrestlers had at least two. There were nudes, cowgirls, knives, guns, horses, tigers, lions, you name it, somebody had a tattoo of it. One boy even had a tattoo of a sailor fighting a Shark, even though the nearest he'd ever been to a Shark was going for wulks down the grassy beach. When it came to tattoos however, nobody got near Janos. He had a snake tattooed right up each arm from wrist to shoulder; a coiled upright ready to strike snake on his back; and on his chest, a snake's head looking forward with its mouth wide open, forked tongue flicking and its two massive pointed fangs dripping venom. According to Janos, the one on his chest alone was worth a round of a start.

The wrestling usually started around eleven o clock in the morning and went on till the last match was finished, usually by three o clock. Problem was, this was also the time Cluny would hold his sermons in the swing park. It was bad enough that the wrestlers and their audience made a bit of a noise at times while he was sermonising, but what probably really bugged Cluny, was the fact that the wrestlers got bigger crowds than him.

At first, Cluny tried the official channels and made a complaint to the council about the misuse of the swing park. As Cluny was a well known greeting face, the council just fobbed him off by saying that something would be done etc. Anyway, nothing was done, and Cluny complained again. This time an official said there wasn't really much he could do. He had looked at the swing park rules and there didn't appear to be any rule against wrestling that he could find. Then Cluny tried going to the Boabees, who in turn said much the same thing, that there was no law against wrestling that they knew of, and that nobody who lived near the swings had made a complaint about noise or disturbance, even daft Margaret. The Inspector that Cluny had went girning to thought he better send Slaberee Alec along to have a look anyway, just in case. For all the good that done, Alec just ended up getting his tunic off and having a go with Janos himself. He actually done better than anybody else, and lasted the whole three rounds, only being beaten by one pinfall. Cluny decided to grin and bear it, but after a couple of weeks he started having the sermons a bit earlier and finished by the time the wrestlers started to turn up. He never forgot it though, and its doubtful whether most folk really knew the depths to which he would stoop to get revenge.

XXIII

Old Bert Campbell had come back to the Rokie from the first world war in 1917, went home to his wife and daughter in Foundry Lane, and never set foot out the door again.

One of the remaining tenements in Foundry Lane was still fully occupied right up till it was demolished. Most of the residents were folk who just couldn't get one of the new council houses for whatever reason. Then there were those who had got one and had been thrown out, again for whatever reason. Then there were folk like Old Bert Campbell who had lived there for what seemed forever, and just didn't want to move.

The young Bert had got married in 1914 at the age of 22, just before the war broke out. Bert had secured the house in Foundry Lane before the wedding, and himself and his new wife had moved in as soon as they had married. A year later, his only child, a daughter, was born. After the war started, Bert had thought about joining up and going off to fight, but he was a skilled man working in one of the city shipyards, and given the impression by his bosses that he could do as much for the war effort by staying at home. There was also the fact that he had just got married, with his wife becoming pregnant soon after. In 1916, after the war had dragged on for two years and had reached a bit of a stalemate, conscription was introduced. Although Bert was exempt on the grounds that he was married and also doing work of national importance, he decided that it was only right that he should go, and so enlisted in the infantry.

It was round fourteen months later that Bert returned home, minus his left leg. But the missing leg was the least of Bert's problems, due to being on the receiving end of continuous bombardment by the German artillery, which resulted in the loss of his leg, his nerves were shattered beyond belief. So bad, that he had spent six months in an army hospital getting himself down to the level of hysterical. Anyway, he had come home after being given a false leg and a small pension from the army, both hopelessly inadequate. Due to his nervous state, Bert was totally unable to resume his old job, or any job for that matter, so his wife went out to work at Halley's

Bert never fully recovered from the damage to his nervous system, but slowly over the years, he did calm down. Most days, he just sat at the fire and stared into space, thinking about god knows what. The house he lived in was one floor up, high enough to look over the Coaly wall. So on good days, Bert would move his chair over to the window, and he could be seen sitting there looking out into the coal yards and over to the docks.

This all sounds innocent enough, but it was to lead to an incident involving my uncle and stepdad that was to set Bert back years.

XXIV

Just before wee Dode got bit by a Crocodile, my uncle and stepdad went on a safari.

It was one of those unusually hot days during the seven weekies when we decided to go fishing down the docks. We dug worms, got the throwie out lines and went to one of the old slipways that went directly into the river. We always went to the old slipways, it meant being right down at the level of the water, not way above it like on the quayside. Whether it was the heat or what, I don't know, but the fish weren't biting that day. Being in the enclosed slipway meant that it was also stifling, and we thought of going for a swim. However, the tide had started to go out, and the water was flying past at some speed. Wee Dode though, was determined to cool off, and took all his clothes off. I warned him not to, as the water was very rapid. He said that he would just hang on to the iron steps at the side of the slip, and climb down them. Fine I thought, his funeral, at sea too. As we were standing there watching him, a lot of debris was being washed past, bits of wood, tree branches and the like. I saw what appeared to be a long tree trunk coming towards us, it was floating just below the surface, had a couple of branches sticking out the sides, and was about ten feet long. All of a sudden, Dode noticed it as it went past him, he gave out a shreik and come flying up the ladder and out on to the slipway. He looked back at the tree trunk, then down at his leg where there was now a couple of scratches, one of them bleeding. ***Ahh*!** He shouted *eh got butt beh i crocodile.*

My uncle Dode and my stepdad Eddie, lived on the top Pletty. They were around the same age, and were both in the TA together. Not having that well a paid jobs, they would often do things together in their spare time that didn't cost either much money or no money at all. This was things like fishing down the docks, going for wulks to the stannergate, walks out to the sticks, or going to the cheap shows. One day, they found a new distraction to fill the time.

One day, my other uncle, home from the navy, came out of Harry Bradley's and spotted two slug guns in the pawn shop window. Could have a bit of fun with them he reckoned, so he went in and bought them. On getting home, he gave me money and instructions to go to a shop in the city centre and buy a whole load of slugs for the guns. Just get what the money will buy he said. I could hardly walk with the weight of them, there was umpteen boxes containing probably enough slugs to wipe out the entire bird population of Europe.

It all started out innocently enough, there we all were, me and Granddad, my wee brothers and cousins and my stepdad and my uncles on the top Pletty firing off slugs at a row of empty cans and bottles placed on the Washhouse roof. However, we soon got fed up of these easy targets, and so any pigeon, sparrow, gull, crow, cat, or for that matter, anything that moved into view was fair game. Of course, it didn't take the local wildlife very long to realise the dangers involved and vanished as soon as anyone was seen on the Pletty. Then Dan Doogan started complaining about the shortage of bottles in the Rokie, so they were put off limits. So the sharpshooters turned to other targets. Before long then, due to the shortage of suitable targets, the novelty of it all wore off and the guns were forgotten about.

One day, my uncle and stepdad, not having any money, and fed up of walking nowhere in particular, were standing having a smoke on the Pletty. They talked about this and that, then when a pigeon appeared on the old school roof, they remembered about the slug guns. They went down to my Grans and raked the guns and ammo out of the press where they had lain for some time.

After a while, the local bird life got wise to what was going on, and went elsewhere till the heat died down. Dode and Eddie stood on the Pletty, guns at the ready for some time before realising there were no living targets. Then Dode, looking over into the Coaly, noticed that there were quite a few birds and rabbits in the place. He took a shot at a rabbit sitting between one of the lines, but it was well out of range. Only one thing for it, they would go and climb over the Coaly wall and go on a safari, if not big game, at least game.

The pair of them went and put on their jackets, not for warmth, but to hide the guns as they walked down the Lane to the Coaly wall. They filled their pockets with slugs, put the guns under their jackets and headed down the stairs into the Lane. Although the Coaly wall was about 8 feet high, there were plenty of places to get over. Bairns were forever going over in to the place to muck about and folk were forever going in to nick coal. Dode and Eddie found a suitable place and after throwing the guns over the wall, they climbed in.

After wandering about for over an hour shooting at anything that moved, they found themselves back at where the wall run along Foundry Lane. The wildlife in the Coaly had all eventually scarpered as the two of them went round shooting, and they hadn't fired the guns for near quarter of an hour. Just as they got to the wall, Eddie noticed a pigeon sitting on a window sill in one of the tenement flats in Foundry Lane that overlooked the Coaly. The window was open, but there didn't seem to be any sign of life. They both took aim at the pigeon and fired off at the same time. One of the slugs slammed right into the pigeon, the feathers flew and the pigeon fell sideways off the sill. The other slug however went through the open window. Now, here's where the whole yarn comes together.

The window in question, was the living room window of one, Old Bert Campbell. Bert often sat at the window looking out on to the Coaly and over to the docks. At the time the slug went through his window, he was sitting at the fireplace staring and day dreaming about nothing in particular. However, just above the fireplace there was a large mirror hanging on the wall. The slug that had missed the pigeon came through the window and hit the mirror. The mirror broke with an almighty smash and went clattering down into the fireplace right where Bert was sitting.

At the sound of this, Eddie and Dode had took off, run along the length of the wall and climbed back over into Foundry Lane. They hid the guns under their jackets and taking a few of the pends had got back to the Close unnoticed. They went up to the top Pletty and into Dode's house. Then using a set of steps they climbed up through the hatch in the loabee and up into the attic. They hid the guns and the slugs amongst some other junk, and then went into the living room and had a game of cards. If anyone asked, they would say they had been playing all afternoon.

An hour or so later, Old Bert's wife got home from work and found him curled up on the floor a quivering wreck.

XXV

One night, just as the pubs were shutting, Slaberee Alec was seen heading out toward Ferry Road in a bit of a hurry. When asked what he was up to, he just said that he was on official police business and he couldn't say anything else. By saying this, Alec was hoping to give an air of importance to his mission, but folk just thought it must be somebody giving out free food somewhere.

He had in fact been told by the sergeant to check out the old disused graveyard on Ferry road for some shenanigans or other that was going on.

Running down the side of the old graveyard, was a lane that went down to the east end of the docks. It was just an unlit dirt track that didn't appear on any map, and had no official name. There was another similar lane across the road that eventually went up to Arbroath Road. There were a few pubs up on Arbroath Road, so the two lanes were quite well used by sailors off the ships that used the docks.

According to the complainer, probably Cluny, the graveyard was being used by local good time girl, Meg Holden, to **hack her mutton** to the sailors. Meg had realised that if she hung around near the graveyard after the pubs shut, there were plenty of customers making their way back to the docks via the lanes. Normally, Alec, or the Sergeant, couldn't care less where Meg done her business, but as somebody had went down to Bell street and moaned about it, he was sent to have a word with her.

When Alec got out to the graveyard, there didn't appear to be anybody around. He had a wander up and down the two lanes for a bit, but all was quiet. He got up on an old tree stump and had a look over the wall of the graveyard, and it too was all quiet. So, he thought he would just sit down on the tree stump and have a smoke before heading back to the Rokie. All going well, he would get back before Dora's Closed.

After finishing his fag, Alec decided to give it another ten minutes or so before heading back. He would tell the sergeant that he staked the place out for an hour or so, and that nothing untoward was going on that he could find. Five minutes later, Alec heard footsteps coming along Ferry road. He sat back a bit and waited to see if anyone would appear. The footsteps got Closer, then stopped just at the head of the lane. Alec looked up the lane, and saw the figure of a woman standing with his back to him. The figure was quite indistinguishable, but Alec knew that it was Meg alright. He decided to wait and see what would happen.

A couple of minutes later, someone came singing and staggering down the top half of the lane. The singer turned out to be a man, probably a sailor off one of the ships. When he crossed the road, he spotted Meg, went up to her and the two of them started talking in low voices. Alec sat and kept quiet, so far Meg hadn't done anything, besides, he was intrigued by the whole episode. Next thing, Meg and the sailor started to walk along Ferry Road. Alec stood up, got up on the tree stump, and had a look over the wall. He could see the tops of their heads moving slowly towards the graveyard gate. They pushed themselves through the gap in the gate, and went in.

Though it was dark, there was just enough light from the street lamps and the moon for Alec to get the general gist of what was going on. Meg and the sailor went over to the big horizontal gravestone, where Meg lay down on her back and pulled up her skirt. The sailor got down on top of her, and after a bit of fumbling about, started to do the deed. Alec should have stepped in some time before they got started, but, he thought, if she got lifted, she'd need the money to pay the fine, so what the hell.

Detective Slabercc investigates

After they were finished, Meg and the sailor got up, adjusting their clothes as they headed toward the gate, and Alec went round to meet them. As they eased through the gap in the gates, they were met by Alec, hands on hips, stern look on his face and an: ***Aye! Aye! Aye! What's been going on here then?*** Both Meg and the sailor were just too stunned to speak and just stood in silence. Alec hooked his thumb over his shoulder and told the sailor to be on his way, which he was only too glad to do.

After the sailor had vanished down the lane, Alec turned to Meg. He started to tell her that he couldn't care less what she did for a living, or in fact where she did it.

But, he told her, a complaint had been made and he had to act on it Blah Blah Blah. All the while that Alec was blethering on, Meg had her hands up the back of her skirt and was rubbing away at her backside. Eventually, Alec asked her what the hell was wrong with her. She said that she didn't know, but that her backside seemed to be covered in marks of some kind. Alec asked her if maybe she had been lying on Ivy or something, that would cause marks and itch like buggery. Meg looked a bit concerned at that, and asked Alec if he would take a look. He said he would, but not out in the street, he had a torch and they would have to go back into the graveyard.

Once in the graveyard, Alec took out his torch and Meg turned round. She hiked up her skirt and Alec hunkered down and pointed the torch at her bare backside. Right enough, he told her, there were some marks there, but he couldn't quite make out what they were. Alec kept shining the torch at Meg's backside, looking at it from various angles. ***Well Sherlock?*** asked Meg, ***any ideas?*** It took a minute or so, but eventually Alec made out just what the marks were, and told her it was writing, backward writing, in fact numbers. Meg asked Alec what the hell he was talking about, what bloody writing? What numbers. Alec then started to laugh to himself, he went over to the grave that Meg and the sailor had been lying on and shone his torch over it. Right enough, there it was, a perfect match, backward: **1914** only on Meg's arse, it said: ᖷIQI

Meg's backside had obviously been lying right on top of the epitaph where it said died in 1914, and that it had been etched temporarily on her arse.

XXVI

Skweebs! The very word must have struck terror into the heart of many an **ald wifey** back in the days when it was totally legal to sell explosives to children.

Just after my birthday in October one year, my uncle John came home from the navy. He had been away for over a year, and as usual, was dripping with money and presents. For Gran and Granddad, he had brought a record player from Japan. Now, I might be wrong about this, but I reckon it was one of the first stereos ever made. The deck was inside a casing that also contained a wireless, and the speakers came off and could be placed away from the deck. Before I knew it, Granddad had his record collection looked out and the house was filled with the sound of Joseph Locke. There were various other presents for aunties and uncles, mainly exotic fags and booze, like Sobrani and Cherry Brandy. For the bairns however, for some reason at his last port of call in Portugal, he had bought a couple of dozen wee flick knives, which he dished out to us. I wont go into detail about this, but it was only a matter of time before Slaberee Alec had confiscated the lot of them, and gave uncle John a word of advice regarding suitable presents for bairns. Uncle John then took me aside and said that as he had missed my last two birthdays, he would give me a little extra present. This was in the shape of a Ten Bob Note. I was rich, rich beyond belief! **Ten Bob!** Not since I robbed that circus midget had I had so much money. This time however, I intended to put it to good use.

It took me half the night and a visit to umpteen shops well away from the Rokie, but I eventually had ten boxes of ten penny bangers. I also bought a box of Swan matches, I reckoned an ordinary box of Bluebells wouldn't be enough for a hundred bangers. I posed the bangers and matches in my posy hole in the boaly, and then went back upstairs to plot my reign of terror.

Next night, once all the gang had assembled: myself, my wee brother, wee cousins and a couple of others including Luca, I told them about the bangers. They were all in raptures at the prospect of some fun with them, and so, like a bunch of terrorists, we set out on our mission. We done the usual throwing bangers up Closes, in bins, in bottles, and even tried to break the chains on the swings with a couple. Then we got daring and threw a couple on to the platform of a passing bus on

Princes Street. We couldn't decide what was best about this, the racket the bangers made, or the sight of the dancing bus conductor as he tried to avoid them. It really was quite amazing watching somebody do the Highland fling in such a confined space, especially with a ticket machine and money bag hanging round their neck. Next was remakes from the show. We had seen a film where a boy blew a safe door open with a stick of dynamite, so we had to try it. There was a suitable keyhole on the door of one of the disused shops on Blackscroft, that'll do we thought. So, a banger in the keyhole, pack it in with some mud out the gutter, light it and stand back. The banger went off, and we had a look at the door. It hadn't opened like in the film, but it had split about a foot up and down from the lock. What next then? What did happen next was to put an end to this particular campaign for some time.

We had a wander up to the top of Halley's Brae to see if anybody was looking for us after the bus caper. At the top of the Brae, there was a wall and some steps. These had been put in because the Brae was so steep, and this would stop cars and lorries trying to use it and getting stuck. We hid down at the corner of the wall and the wall of the Bakery that was also at the top of the Brae. We were plotting our next move when somebody came running up the Brae towards us. When the somebody got Close, I realised it was my older cousin, Jake. His mum, who was my Mother's older sister, was over visiting my Gran and Granddad, and he had been brought along. Jake was a well known terrorist in the area he lived, and when he heard the bangers going off, had put two and two together and came looking for us. He asked me for a banger and a couple of matches, which I gave him. He then pulled a roll of insulating tape out of his pocket that he said he got out of Granddads tool box. Jake then told us to wait where we were, and ran across the road to the other side of Princes Street. On the other side, there was a shop with a big window, much bigger than the other shops. Jake taped the banger to the window, lit it and came running back across to where we were. Seconds later, there was the usual bang, but this was accompanied by a loud crack. It was dark and the streetlights were too dim to let us see what had happened. Next thing however, we found out when a huge triangular bit of glass fell out of the window frame and crashed on to the pavement. It took us a few seconds to recover from the shock of the unbelievable racket from the window, then we just turned and run. Before I even got back to the Close, I knew the game was up with the bangers, so I waited till the rest had went home then hid what was left of them in the boaly.

    I had been right enough about the game being up with the bangers. For a good few days after the shop window nonsense, not just Slaberee Alec, but a couple of other Boabees, even ones in disguise were seen lurking around. Never mind, I thought, they'll keep till next year.

    Also a great malarkey with squeebs was rockets, especially when, like bangers, they get used in every way but the right way.

When they were round eight years old, two boys, twins, came to stay in one of the big houses along Ferry Road. Their names were Eck and Billy, and after getting to know us from school, they started to come along to the Rokie most nights to play with us. They were originally from some remote hole in the country where their old man was a big shot in some job. He had got another big shot job in the city, and so Eck, Billy, their mum, dad, and their Granddad had moved here. Their old Granddad as it turns out, was a world champ ginger snap eater. Being married to a successful man, their Mother had adopted some serious airs and graces, but their dad and Granddad were just choochters at heart. Eck and Billy pulled a stunt with some rockets one time that gave them not only great status among us, but also gave them their nicknames.

This came about one night when they tried to make a bazooka, like the ones on the American war fims. Basically, the pair of them had tied a bunch of thrupenny rockets together, twisted all the fuse papers into one and stuffed the lot up a length of four inch drainpipe. Eck had mounted the pipe on his shoulder and aimed it at a window in a derelict tenement, just like a GI in a war film aiming at a German tank. Billy had lit the fuse paper, and a few seconds later sparks started flying out the back end of the pipe. Next thing, the whole lot started to move up the pipe at about three miles and hour, but all of a sudden, just as the rockets got to the front end of the pipe, they suddenly took off. Problem is, rockets are designed to go straight up the way, not horizontally, so, as soon as they came out the pipe, they performed a sort of arc, and hit the ground a few feet away. But, they didn't just stop there, the thrust kept them going and they started to bounce off anything in their way and keep going at an alarming rate. To make matters worse, the string holding the rockets together broke, and so they all flew off in different directions. Thing was, the brothers were in a back green area of an old tenement and surrounded by walls. For what seemed like forever, but was in fact just a few seconds, the rockets screamed back and forward at all angles as they kept bouncing off walls.

After the rockets had run out of thrust and finally stopped, the brothers got up out of the curled up positions they had dived into and surveyed the scene. The rockets, which were all over the place, were still smoking and a couple of them had come to a stop just a couple of feet from where they were now standing, another second of thrust and they would have been hit. Not that it would have made any difference, the two of them looked like they had been dropped down a lum into a burning fireplace. Their faces were blackened and their eyebrows and hair all singed, in fact Eck's hair was still smoking. The front of both their jerseys were black and covered in small holes which were still burning, obviously made by the millions of sparks from the rockets as they came out the pipe. The air was thick and acrid with the smoke from the rockets, and there was also a whiff of burnt wool and hair. Me and the others, who had been watching from a safe distance, had got over the shock of the event and had now run over to the pair of them. We all jabbered ten to the dozen about what had happened, what had went wrong and what could be done to improve the design. But the brothers were more concerned about what they were going to tell their mum about how they got in such a state, particularly the state of their now burned to a crisp school jerseys. What did they do? Well, on the way home, they stopped and had a wash in a dub, dried themselves with their jerseys, then threw them away. We walked with them as far as the door of their house, then knowing their mums ferocious reputation, we left them to it.

We never found out what happened when they got in the house that day, but apart from school, we didn't see the brothers out and about for a while after that. The name stuck though, although they got called by their first names, together, they always got referred to as the Bazooka brothers.

XXVII

Uncle John had some strange ideas when it came to bringing back presents for the bairns from his sojourns, but one time, he really surpassed himself.

We were out in the backies one day, and had set up a Trapeze under the bottom Pletty. We had been to see the film, The Greatest Show on Earth, and were now trying out a Flying Trapeze act for ourselves. The 'Trapeze'' consisted of two bits of washing line and a bit of wood hung from the Pletty, which was just a swing. The act consisted of standing on a bin at the Close back entrance, then swinging under the Pletty. After a while, we had got daring and hung another 'Trapeze'' further along the Pletty. We had got to the bit where we would swing out and try to change over from one swing to the next, generally ending up falling on our backs as we did. Wee Dode had really taken to this malarkey, and had taken off his sark and put on a pair of wee Tam's short breeks over his jeans. The shorts were far too wee for him, but along with his vest, he felt he looked the part of Cornel Wilde, the Trapeze artist in the film. It had just got to the interesting bit, where Dode was going to attempt to grab my hands and let me swing him under my swing. The fact that the swings were only five feet off the ground didn't seem to enter into the equation. Just as I started to swing out to meet him, uncle John appeared at the Close back entrance.

Uncle John had only been away for around 6 months, which for him was a short trip. We were always glad to see him, mainly because he always brought back presents, and this time was to be no exception as he was laden down with parcels. To a boy, we all rushed to him and started dancing around his feet. He dished out the packages and said to help him up the stairs with them, which we gladly did, shaking the boxes to see if we could tell what was in them. It was obvious Gran and Grandddad weren't expecting uncle John, as there was a lot of hugging and shrieks of surprise when he got to their door. We were all told to go and get the rest of the family down to the house, and a couple of minutes later the house was full of goodwill, and drink.

The drink was in the shape of bottles of spirits, mostly flavoured Schnapps which was for my aunties and uncles, and for Granddad a bottle of a stuff called Stroh. This Stroh was a bottle of flavoured Rum, something Granddad had a taste for from his Navy days. Granddad went and got a glass and poured himself a large drink of the Stroh, which he downed in two gulps. He then poured another glassful, and sat back to enjoy it. Ten minutes later, he had the record player out and the sounds of Beniamino Gigli were drowned out by Granddad joining in at the top of his voice. It must be strong stuff I thought, and picked up the bottle. A look at the label told me that this stuff, Stroh, was 90% proof, and the fact that it was also only meant as a flavouring additive for the likes of jam and cakes. Granddad had just drank the equivalent of 14 nips and was blootered. I told my Gran, who took the bottle and posed it in the coal bunker.

Once everybody, aunts, uncles, great aunts and cousins were all gathered, uncle John dished out the rest of the goodies. For Gran, he had brought a cuckoo clock, something she had wanted for a long time. However, whether she would want this particular clock, was another thing. When the clock struck the hour, the cuckoo came out and gave out its cuckoo, cuckoo as expected, but it had a little added extra. This was in the shape of a woman standing there in a long voluminous skirt, when the cuckoo came out, so did a little man who pulled the woman's skirt up revealing a pair of patched bloomers. At first, Gran was a bit taken aback by this, but when my great auntie Maisy said they were just like Belle's drawers, she gave out a laugh and decided she liked it. Great auntie Belle wasn't to amused at first, but a couple of Apricot Schnapps soon took care of that.

It was when the bairns presents were revealed though, that things took a downward turn, for us bairns anyway. Uncle John really had some strange ideas for presents for us, but this was taking the piss. He opened a couple of parcels and took out what to us was 5 pairs of leather shorts with shoulder straps. Uncle John then told us they were in fact called Lederhosen, or to us, leather breeks. But that wasn't the end of it though, oh no, not by a long shot it wasn't. He opened another parcel and hauled out 5 hats. These hats were like the hat Louie the Next wore, but smaller. The hats also had a head band with a feather sticking out of it. Now that the adults were all a bit tipsy with the foreign drink, apart from Granddad, who by this time was speaking in tongues, it was suggested we try on the outfits. We were sent into the back room, and once there we took our breeks off and got into the Lederhosen, or rather, on my part, struggled to get into them. The problem was, the five of us ranged in size from me at near 5 feet, to wee Tam who was about 3 feet, while the Lederhosen were all the same bloody size. Being about three sizes too small, the hems of mine came right up to my crotch and tucked in just below my arse cheeks. Dode's were also too wee, but not as wee as mine, while Ronnie and Davy's were about the right size. Wee Tam's however, had to be seen to be believed. The opposite of mine, they were about three sizes too big, with the hems trailing the floor. A voice from the other room then asked if we were ready, and too come through to the front room. We all marched in to the front room and stood in a line. My Gran and auntie Belle both said we looked cute, while the rest were all falling about laughing. I honestly thought my auntie Maisy was going to piss herself she was laughing so much. I wasn't amused though, especially as my balls were being crushed to a pulp with the hideous things. After they had all had a good laugh, we trooped back to the back room and got changed again. All except wee Tam that is.

Once in the back room, I felt a rush of relief at getting the Lederhosen off and getting back into my jeans. Same with the hat, it was of very course material and my head was sweating and itching. The rest said much the same, except Tam, who just refused point blank to take either off. ***They're fae Austria!*** he shouted, as if that gave them some kind of credibility. Then I thought, how does he know where there from. I asked him, and he said that his dad, my stepdad, had told him. Okay! I said and thought nothing more of it. For the next god knows how long, Tam had these leather breeks and the hat on, he even wore them with his cowboy guns, and even to his bed. It was a sight and a half looking out into the backies and seeing all the youngest bairns playing. They'd be wearing the stuff 3 and 4 year old bairns usually wear, jeans, Sloppy Joes, and the like, so it was quite amazing to see among this scene of normality, a 4 year old wearing a massive pair of Lederhosen and a Tyrolean hat.

That wasn't the end of the saga though. Later on that afternoon, I asked my stepdad about the Austria connection with the breeks and hats. As he was explaining to me about Lederhosen, yodelling and the like, my Granddad who had sobered up a bit, perked up his ears suddenly. He asked where the Rum was, and went and got it. He looked at the label, then checked the labels on the various bottles of Shnappes. Granddad then turned to uncle John and asked what the hell he was doing in bloody Austria, **its hunders i miles fae the sea** he said to him.

Lederhosen fashion show

The story that eventually unfolded was like something out of a Humphrey Bogart/Lauren Bacall film. Uncle John had been on a cruise ship that was working the Mediterranean, and had docked in Genoa in Italy. He had met a British army nurse there, and had had a fling with her for the few days he was there. He had then sailed for ports in Greece and Egypt, returning to Genoa two weeks later. He looked up the nurse, and she told him that not only was she pregnant, she had been posted to a hospital in Austria. On hearing all this, uncle John then stayed with her for a couple of days, then joined his ship for one last cruise. He handed in his notice, and on his return headed to Austria to join the nurse. When he met up with her, he declared his undying love, then took a job on a cruise boat that was working the Danube. It didn't work out however, while he was on a weeks cruise of the river, the nurse met up with someone else, and that was the end of it. Hence the Austrian presents, and I suppose an Austrian cousin.

XXVIII

So, I'm sitting at the table trying to eat soup with a fork. Given that my Gran's soup is very thick, not as much a problem as might be thought. My Gran however, is giving me some very serious looks. Eventually, she cant hold it back anymore, ***kin yi no yaze a spane like abdee else,*** she says to me venomously. I attempt to say something, but am halted by the ominous look my Granddad is giving me. He was sitting across from me, eating his soup with a spoon. It was a look that said, ***dare, jist blidee dare.*** I quickly picked up the bowl, and drained the rest of the soup, most of it going over my face. Gran told me to go and wash myself and get the hell out to play, with a comment that as we lived at the docks, maybe I should run away to sea.

What was this all about? Well! One Saturday, my Gran, mum and aunties all decided to go into town shopping. This meant they'd be gone all day. Granddad said that Captain Scott's Antarctic expedition didn't take as long as one of their Saturday shopping sprees. As my uncle and stepdad had decided to go to the match, Granddad was left to keep an eye on us lot.

We decided to go down to Foundry Lane to play pigeon tennis and got the gear out. This was apart from Tam, my youngest brother who was only three and a half. He had stayed to play round the backies with the other bairns his age, which usually involved digging holes or the like.

A good while later, we had wearied of pigeon tennis. Pigeon tennis? Basically, you put some bread out in a quiet street like Foundry Lane, hide behind a wall, then when the pigeons come down for the bread, you run out and whack one of them up the arse with a tennis racquet. So, the score was 13-0 us, the pigeons had deserted the area, and it was taking longer and longer between setts, so we headed back to the Close.

When we got to the Close, Tam and the other laddies were deeply involved in a game which involved the contents of one of the bins round the Backies. Tam bent over to pick something up, and I noticed a bulge in the erse of his short trousers. I went over and gave his erse a poke and realised that he had shit his breeks. Not only that, he had obviously done it some time before, and some of it had run down his leg and hardened. He was probably so involved in the game, he couldn't be bothered going up to get the lavee key, and after doin it, knew what he was in for.

    I got hold of him, and took him upstairs to Granddad, getting called for everything as I did. Its amazing just how much swearing a bairn of his age knew. We got to the house and Granddad was not amused at getting his afternoon of wireless and papers disturbed. He was also just getting stuck into his favourite snack, 8 or 9 Ginger Snaps dropped into a mug of tea and supped with a spoon. Granndad took Tam over to the sink, stood him on the bunker and pulled his breeks off. As the shite on his arse and legs was by now quite hard, Granddad put some water in the basin, then sat Tam in it to soften it up. He then took Tam's breeks and run them under the well. Some of the shite wouldn't shift, so, what Granddad did next was to have a profound effect on me for years to come. He reached over and took a spoon out of the cutlery tray on the bunker, then used it to scrape the shite of the breeks. After he was done, he run the spoon under the well, gave it a dry on the curtains and put it back in the tray. *AAAAAAAHHHHH!!!* Went though my head, what spoon was it, I thought. I looked through the spoons in the tray but there was loads of them. I asked Granddad if he knew what spoon it was, as I didn't ever want to use it. He just said ***whuts wrang wi yi? Its only shite.***

XXIX

It all started when my great auntie Belle came up to the house and told my Granddad that one of their nieces was getting married. This niece was the daughter of one of my Grandads other sisters, Jenny, and her husband Jeck. Turns out, it was going to be in the High Kirk, with a reception in the fanciest hotel in the city.

My Granddad sat all through this, then asked just what it had to do with him. Belle told him that it was his niece and so he would be expected to go. Granddad said to Belle that he doubted he'd be invited, as he had fallen out with Jenny some time before.

This fall out happened at a tea and peeces session at Jenny's house following a christening one Sunday. My uncle John, who hadn't been invited, sent one of the bairns into the house to ask his Granny (Jenny) what a dangleberry is. Not having a clue what uncle John's talking about, the bairn disappears into the house. Having fallen for the same thing myself, I followed him. He runs into the room where they all sat, and in a loud voice says **Gran, whats a dangleberry?** Hear a pin drop, you could have heard a flea farting. The silence lasted a few seconds, then a voice from next to the fire pipes up and everybody looks round. My Granddad, sitting staring into the fire munching on a piece, without even looking up says **It's a wee ba i shite that sticks ti the hairs on yir erse.** Next thing Jeck, who was taking a drink of his tea, explodes into his cup as he lets out a suppressed laugh. Then to cap it all, my great auntie Maisy, one of my Granddads other sisters, gives out a long high pitched cackle. She sounded like a hen laying an extra large egg. At this, everybody sits with embarrassed grins and tries to look like this is something normal. Jenny however, sits and gives Granddad the filthiest look imaginable. You could see the poison dripping out of her eyes. And that's the story of the fallout.

So, Granddad and auntie Jenny haven't spoken since, not that they had much to say to each other before anyway. It seems however, that Belle had spoken to Jen about this, and Granddad was going to be invited. So, Belle tells him, he'll have to buy a new suit and shoes and what have you. This is where the tricky bit comes in.

If there's one thing Granddad hates spending money on, its clothes. This hatred went especially for fancy clothes, like suits. To him, a suit should last forever, perhaps longer. He did have a suit, and it obviously had lasted forever judging by the look of it. He went and raked it out of the wardrobe and showed it to Belle. The trouser bottoms were a bit frayed, while the seat was sagging in the traditional style, halfway to the knees. The jacket wasn't too bad, but there was a few fag burns here and there, and what I took to be a big beer stain down one of the lapels. Belle's reaction to this was that he couldn't possibly wear that to a fancy wedding like this one, especially not in the High Kirk. It was simple, she told him he'd have to buy a new one, and she'd give him the money. Nope, he told her, if she wanted him to get a new suit, she could go and get it herself. He was a 34 waist and a 40 chest, pattern, colour and cloth was up to her. As for shoes, don't bother, he had a pair of good shoes and they would do fine. He went and got them and showed her just how fine a pair they were. He had got them some time in the distant past, and they were only ever used for special occasions, so they were in fine condition. And they were, she agreed.

These shoes were Granddad's pride and joy. He had been issued with them in the Navy when he served in the first world war. Now, Navy standard issue dress shoes really are something else. They are hand cut and stitched by the best shoemaking firms in the country, from the absolute best leather to be found. A pair of these shoes, if looked after, will last forever, and boy had Granddad looked after them. They had been spit and polished till they gleamed, and you really could see your face in them. Some nights, when he had nothing else to do, Granddad would take them out of the wooden box he had made to keep them and his other Navy memorabilia in, and polish them, even though they were already shining.

Although they were his pride and joy, Granddad had no problems in lending them out to anybody he trusted for special occasions. Only a few weeks earlier, my stepdad had borrowed them for a job interview, and before that, my uncle Dode had wore them to a mates wedding. It would be very interesting to chronicle a history of these shoes. From what I could gather from the people who had used them and from Granddads recollections, the shoes indeed had a distinguished history. They had been on parades before King George V and the King of Egypt, had travelled tens of thousand of miles and been present at the battle of Jutland and the bombardment of Alexandria. They had been at approximately 14 weddings, 17 christenings, and had danced every dance from the Pas a Dobles and the Tango to Strip the Willow and the Dashing White Sergeant. They had also been in around 10 fights, and had appeared in court at least three times. They had also graduated twice from the university with degrees in law and civil engineering. This was courtesy of two students who had worked in the sawmills beside Granddad during the summer.

As for the suit, well, Granddad later said to my Gran, if she wants to waste good money on one, fine, she's obviously got more money than sense. Now, any man in the Rokie would simply go to the pawn shop, get a suit, wear it to the wedding or whatever, then take it back and get some money for it. If the pawn didn't have anything suitable, then upstairs to Louie the Next to see what he had. Not auntie Belle though, oh no, she went to the best, most expensive tailors in town. Only problem was, she just didn't have a clue what she was in for price wise.

Once she saw the prices in this particular shop, she changed her mind about buying the suit there, and was on her way out the door when something caught her eye. It was May, and so there was a rack of heavy wool winter suits going at half price. She had a rake through them and found what she was looking for, a dark green 3 piece serge suit, 34 waist breeks, 40 chest jacket and waistcoat. It was perfect, she thought, and took it to the desk and handed over the money.

Now, if there was one other thing my Granddad hated next to spending good money on suits, it was wearing wool next to his skin. He took one feel off the cloth, and said there was no way he was wearing it, he'd be clawing all day. Well, said Belle and my Granny, he would just have to wear his long drawers with it, then he wouldn't notice. He went into the next room and put the suit trousers over his long drawers. He came back through and said it was okay, a bit heavy, but it would do, he supposed. Well, that seemed to be the end of that auld sang, as somebody once said. But, the saga of this particular suit was far from over.

A couple of months later, the wedding took place and all seemed to go well with everybody saying they had a great time at the reception. Everybody but Granddad that is. The wedding was at the end of July on one of the hottest days anybody could remember. Fine for the wedding and those concerned, but for Granddad in his heavy serge suit and long drawers, it had been a nightmare. Things hadn't been too bad at the Kirk which was an old stone building that was always cold, even on hot days like that. But once back at the reception, what with a hot day, a hall with hardly any windows and the lights blazing, Granddad started to feel the heat. As the day went on, all he could do was sit and stew in his get up. After a few drams, the accordions started his feet tapping, so he tried getting up for a Strip the Willow, his favourite dance. A couple of minutes later, with the sweat dripping of him, he disappeared into the toilets for a good half hour. Uncle Jeck was sent to look for him, and found him in a cubicle with his jacket off, waistcoat open and his breeks and drawers around his ankles. Jeck said that it was some shite he was having to take this length of time. He wasn't having a shite though, he told Jeck, he was just trying to cool down.

That night when he got home, Granddad swore that that was the last time he ever wore that bloody suit. He hung it in the wardrobe and vowed to get rid of it somehow. It would have to be before another doo came up, and in a way that would seem not to be his fault, without arousing Belle's suspicions. It took a while, but he did eventually find a way.

Granddads first move in getting rid of the suit, was to take it to the pawn and leave it there till the pledge ticket ran out. That way, old man Cohen would sell it, he'd be rid of it, and he would just claim that he forgot about it. Not as easy as might be thought though. A few months after he pawned the suit, and only a few days before the pledge ran out, Gran found the ticket and went along to the shop and redeemed it. Granddad was absolutely gobsmacked when he went into the wardrobe one day looking for a clean sark, and found the suit hanging there, staring at him defiantly. He asked my Gran about it, and she said she found the ticket, and thought that maybe he had forgot it, so she better get it out, seeing there was only had a couple of days left on the ticket. Shite, he thought, only a couple of days and he'd have been rid of the bloody thing. Not just that, Tam and Jen's youngest daughter and her lad had just declared undying love, so it was only a matter of time before another wedding came up. But, help was at hand in the shape of Dan Doogan.

One night, a couple of weeks later, Dan Doogan came into Harry Bradley's and said he had just had a court summons, and was due to appear in about three weeks. He'd been nabbed red handed filling bottles out of a bubbling, hissing still in an old Washhouse in Foundry Lane. He said he intended to plead guilty, and throw himself on the mercy of the court. Sticky Tam said he'd been watching too many episodes of Perry Mason. Dan reckoned that if he said the right things and looked the part, he might get off with a fine. After all, it was only his 17th offence, and the first time for distilling without a licence. He told Louie the Next that he would be up to see him about a new suit the next day.

At the mention of suit, my Granddads ears pricked up. A thought went though his head, and he mulled it over. If he gave Dan a loan of the suit, and Dan got the jail, which he surely would, he would be taken from the court, in the suit, right to the jail, directly to the jail, he would not pass go, he would not collect 200 pounds, and the suit would go with him. Granddad went over and joined Dan at the bar. He told him not to waste good money on a suit, he had just the thing for him.

A couple of weeks later, despite his court summons, Dan was back at the whisky business. He had found another old Washhouse and had set up a still and what have you. After all, he had said, if he was going to get fined, he'd need the money to pay it. A few hours into the distilling process, Dan was sitting having a fag and waiting for the first few drops to come through. Then he noticed a strange noise coming from the still, and stood up to go and have a look. Before he took a step, there was an almighty bang, and the still blew up. Dan, standing in front of the open door was blown of his feet, through the door and landed on his arse a few feet from the Washhouse. Then what happened next, was just pure bad luck. The Washhouse roof was blown in the air with the force of the explosion, performed an arc, and landed right on top of Dan.

Slaberee Alec on duty

Slaberee Alec, who was standing round the back of old man Tyree's eating a bridie, heard the bang of the still going up. He looked in the general direction of the bang, and saw what he took to be either steam or smoke rising a couple of hundred yards away. Taking his bridie with him, Alec set off to investigate.

When he got to where the still had blown up, Alec found the remains of the Washhouse, plus the remains of the Washhouse roof lying a few yards away. He had a look inside the wrecked Washhouse, saw the remains of the still and knew that it had just been Dan at his old capers. As he walked past the roof, he saw what he knew to be Dan's wooden hand sticking out from beneath the slates and bits of wood. He tried to pick up the hand, and found it was attached to something. He pulled and an arm came out a bit. it was only then that Alec realised what the hand was attached too. It was Dan's arm.

The result of all this, was that Dan was now Dan Doogan. Distiller. Deceased.

A few days later, on Saturday afternoon there was a knock at the door. I went to answer it, and found that there was a small delegation from Harry Bradley's standing there. Harry, Sticky Tam, Frankie McPhee, Tinky McLairen, Daft Johnny and a few others. Sticky Tam said they were going up to the catholic church a few streets away, to see, and pay respects to the mortal remains of Dan Doogan. It was a good day, so Granddad just went as he was in his cardigan and slippers. I asked to go as well, and he said okay.

The coffin in which Dan had been placed was in a side room off the main church. He was to be buried on the following Tuesday, so he was put there till a mass was said on the Monday night, then taken back to the house for a traditional wake. They all went in to the room, one by one they said their piece to him, and filed out again. When I went to leave the room also, Granddad grabbed me by the shoulder and held me there next to him. I looked up wondering what was wrong. He was covering his mouth with his hand, and his head and shoulders were shaking. I thought at first he was crying, but also thought that was a bit strange, as he wasn't all that good a friends with Dan. Then he took his hand away from his face and I could see that he had a huge smile on his face, and that he was shaking with laughter. What could be so funny, I thought. I couldn't see very well over the side of the coffin, and tried standing on tiptoe. Then Granddad lifted me up and I got a full view of the dead Dan lying there. I still couldn't figure out what was so funny though. There were a few marks on Dan's face where the mortician had tried to cover up the injuries from the blast at the Washhouse, but apart from that? Then Granddad asked me what was he wearing? Then it dawned on me, Dan was wearing Granddads hated suit.

It turns out, that Dan's brother, Jim, had been informed of his death, and had travelled up from his home somewhere in England to take care of the arrangements, and sort out his affairs. It seems that getting buried in your best clothes is a tradition of some sort where Dan came from. So Jim, finding the suit in the house and presuming it was Dan's, had given it to the Undertaker.

So there was Dan, lying in the coffin in my Granddads best, but hated and unwanted suit. What a result, once it and Dan were buried, there was no chance he would ever see the thing again. And he just couldn't wait to see the look on Belle's face when he told her. Let her try and work out how to get it back again. ***Honest Your Honour, I was just digging up the grave to get my brother's suit back.*** Then, he looked down at the rest of Dan and his face fell. I too looked down and saw the cause of this. There at the bottom end of the coffin, on Dan's feet, were Granddads precious shoes. Grandad had forgot that beside the suit, he'd gave Dan a loan of the shoes.

By this time, the rest of the mourners were getting impatient waiting for Granddad. They were going to the pub to plan the wake, and wanted to know if he was going or not. Granddad said just to go on ahead without him, as he was wanting to go and find Father Mahon, to have a word with him about some Rhubarb he was growing. Once they had all left the church, Granddad went back into the side room. He took the shoes off Dan's feet, then pulled his slippers off and put them in their place. He pulled the coffin lining and the hems of the suit breeks down and around Dan's feet, making them less noticeable. Granddad then put the shoes on and said to me, lets get the hell out of here, as somebody once said.

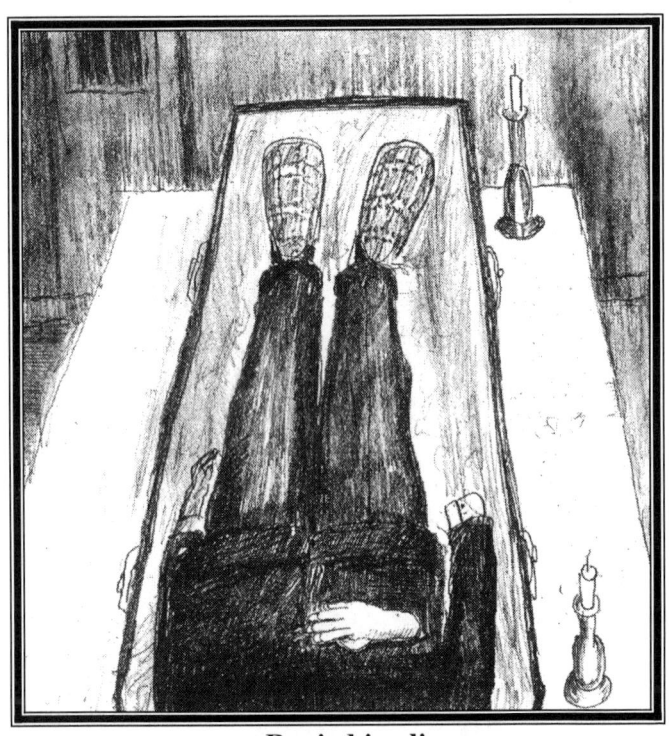

Buried in slippers

That was more or less the story of the suit. It turned out that Granddad didn't have to wait for Dan to get buried to see the end of it. At the wake, everybody got so pissed that it was more like a wedding. Around about two in the morning, somebody had went into the room where the coffin had been put. They were so pissed, they must have been falling about and knocked some candles over that were on a table next to the coffin. The candles had fallen into the coffin and set fire to the lining. It took a bit of time before anybody noticed the smoke coming from under the door, and by that time, the coffin and Dan were well ablaze. The drunk crowd at the wake had managed to put the fire out with water from the kitchen, but it was to late. Dan's body wasn't burned right through, but it was pretty badly charred. As for the suit though, it was burned to a crisp. The outcome of all this however, was that Dan became probably the first man in history to be half cremated and half buried.

XXX

After the demise of Miss Pearson, we had to put up with the Haidee for a few days. This meant having to do what we were supposed to be doing in the first place, learning. There was no doubt the Haidee was a dedicated and experienced teacher, but he was such a bore. Everything was about schoolwork, whether it was sums, reading, or even what we usually enjoyed, like crafts or art, somehow, the Haidee would turn it into an effort that just turned us off. There was also the fact that the Haidee was a religious maniac. No matter what the subject, he would manage to turn it into a study of the bible. For instance, an arithmetic lesson one day was based on the size of Noah's bloody Ark. That and stopping for a "moment" of prayer every hour, we couldn't wait to see the back of him. One day, we did.

A week or so later, we went into the class one morning and found a new teacher sitting at the desk. Miss Clarke, as she introduced herself. Miss Clarke was the opposite of Pearson, she was young, maybe too young to be in with us rif raf. Again, I found out years later that she was a trainee teacher.

There was a teacher training college in Dundee, and due to the shortage of teachers, she was allowed in to a school to finish her last year.

To say she was a plain Jane, is a bit of an understatement. She had short frizzy hair, big black rimmed specs, and dressed like she was on a Sunday school picnic. She was wearing a long flowery print skirt to well under her knees, a short black jacket, and a pair of shoes that wouldn't have been out of place in an army parade. When she got round to speaking, it was with a deliberately assertive, aggressive voice. She wasn't fooling us though, we picked up right away that it was an act. She laid down the rules she expected us to follow, and what would happen if we broke them. To accentuate this, she took out a belt from the desk drawer and brought it clattering down on the desktop. It was this belt that was to lead to her downfall.

For the next few weeks, Miss Clarke did her best to batter us into submission. By we, I mean the boys in the class, the girls were treated with courtesy and called by their first names. But us laddies, we were treated like convicts on a chain gang. It was all second or full names, and the slightest thing it was so and so, OUT! Wallop. But the more she did, the more we took the piss. Homework wasn't done, but she never noticed because it was never handed in, art lessons turned into chaos as we painted each other and everything but the paper, sitting playing games like truth dare, and general mayhem. Best of the lot was when she brought a bucket full of clay in to the class. She said pottery, and making things with clay was her hobby, and she had a wheel and a kiln at home. If we made some nice things with the clay, she would take them home and fire them. Fine, what we ended up with was the usual nice items such as copies of ornaments at home, clay dogs, cats and the like, and a dozen clay laddies knobs. That was the last of the pottery classes. It was also after this that she said: ***Right, I'm putting the foot down!***

It turns out her idea of putting the foot down meant a change of tactic with the belt. For weeks, she had dished it out mercilessly, and it hadn't had the slightest effect on us. From now on, she announced, anyone doing anything that would have meant the belt, would still get the belt. But! The offender would bend over her desk and receive it over the arse. This of course, caused a lot of chuckles, sniggers and whispers. If she thought this would make any difference, she would be right, but difference to who.

Things went on as normal for the rest of that day. We carried on as usual, but the threat wasn't carried out. Whether she was waiting on the right offence or offender, it was hard to tell, but by the end of the day, nobody had a sore arse. The next day was the same, till around eleven o clock. This was when the teachers collected the dinner money. A pal of mine, big Dode, was sitting at his desk, when Miss Clarke asked a girl sitting behind him to bring her money to her desk. The girl gets up, starts to walk down the aisle past Dode's desk, and as she does, he reaches out his hand and pulls the back of her skirt up. She lets out a scream, and pulls her skirt down again. Of course, Miss Clarke wants to know what happened, and the girl is only too willing to provide the details.

This is deemed to be a serious enough offence to merit the belt over the arse. Dode gets called out as she takes her belt out of the drawer. She then tells him to bend over her desk, and raises the belt. Now this is where the interesting bit comes in. Dode, like a few other laddies, is wearing short breeks, and like a few other laddies, his are made of heavy blue serge, the stuff uniforms are made off. So, the belt goes up, comes down on Dode's backside, and a big cloud of stoor shoots of it. She obviously intended to give him a couple more, but after the roar of laughter that went up at the first stroke, she thought better of it, and told Dode to go back to his seat. He told us later, that probably due to the thickness of his breeks, along with his **drars,** he never felt a thing.

Anyway, the outcome of this was that next day, we had the Haidee in the class again. That was also the last we ever saw of Miss Clarke.

XXXI

Shug the Thug wasn't the only pet my Granddad had though. There was also the King of Egypt.

One time, my Gran and my Granddad's sisters all went on some kind of bus jaunt out to the country, something to do with some daft club or other they were all in. Anyway, they went to a village in some remote hole or other where they were having a fete or the like. My Gran had always fancied keeping a couple of hens, and my Granddad had agreed to build her a henhouse on the allotment if she ever did. So, she asks this farmer she meets at the fete about this, and he says that the best way was to take a couple of ready to hatch eggs home with her. He sells her three eggs, two average size ones, and one about twice the size. The farmer tells her that its bigger because it's a cockerel's egg, and if she's going to keep hens she'll need a cockerel. What the hell does she know, she just takes his word for it and takes the eggs home. If she follows the farmers instructions to keep the eggs warm, in a couple of days, they'll hatch.

So, there we are, me, Granddad and Gran, sitting by the fire, waiting on the eggs hatching. Gran had put the eggs in an old hat of hers that she'd lined with straw, and sat in the hearth of the fireplace. We sat patiently all day and evening, watching for the faintest sign of life from the eggs. Later that night, right enough, the two smaller eggs hatched out and there were two of the cutest little chicks you could ever see. Granddad put them in a Peek Freans Assortment biscuit tin he had looked out, and we fed them on bits of bread. The big egg however, just sat there in the hat, not moving and no sign of anything happening.

I must have eventually fallen asleep and been put to bed, cos next thing I knew I was waking up there. I got up, went through to the front room, looked in the hearth and there was no third egg. My Gran told me that the egg had hatched during the night and the chick was in the biscuit tin. Well, something was in the biscuit tin, but even I could tell that it didn't come from any bloody hen. For a start, it was twice the size of the two chicks and was pure white. But the real giveway wasn't just the fact that this thing had webbed feet and a bright orange bill instead of a beak, it also didn't go cheep, it gave off a very faint but very distinct honk.

Whether the farmer did what he did out of bad mindedness or whether he just had a good sense of humour, we never found out. We also never found out what kind of goose it was, but a goose it was okay, and going to be a bloody big one before long too.

My Gran kept the chicks and the gosling in the house for a couple of weeks. It was amazing how quick they grew, and just how much they could eat, especially the Gosling. It was also amazing just how much shite could come out of something so small too. So, after a couple of weeks, my Granddad took the three of them down to the allotment where he had built the promised henhouse. Problem was, he had built the thing to a set of plans he had got out of the Rokie Library. Plans that didn't take into account the fact that the hens would have a lodger, a big lodger who wouldn't be able to fit through any of the doors in a couple of months.

Everything was ok for a while after that, the problem with the door never materialised because the goose preferred not to use the henhouse, and instead spent all its time outside. Granddad was highly delighted with this arrangement, because as the goose got bigger, it also got scarier. Within a couple of months, the goose had become fully grown, and was nearly as big as Jimmy James the midget, who was now so scared of the thing that he wouldn't even walk along the pavement past the allotment. Granddad had occasionally had trouble with folk nicking his logs, or vegetables from his garden, but that looked like a thing of the past. Anybody coming near the place was met with the sight and sound of the goose flapping its huge wings and honking like a dervish. It was in fact better than any guard dog he had said.

Then, a big mistake was made, at least as far as the goose was concerned. The hens and the goose were given names. It had always been the intention to get a cockerel, and only keep the hens for the eggs, so naming them was never going to be an issue. So, from somewhere or other, my Gran managed to get hold of a cockerel. Probably the cockerel shop, as my Granddad had told her when she first asked where she could get one. The cockerel was named Victor, after Victor Mature of Samson and Delilah fame, and the hens were called Maisy and Daisy after my Granddad's two older sisters nicknames, after all he said, they look like them, so why not. My Gran wanted to call the goose Donald, simple as that, but my Granddad had other ideas.

One of my Granddad's heroes, was King Farouk of Egypt. According to Granddad, he had once met the King of Egypt. A tall tale indeed, but what had actually happened was: During his days as a sailor with the Royal Navy Reserve, the Wavy Navy, the ship he was on had called at the port of Alexandria in Egypt. The sailors had all been on parade on the dockside and been presented to King

Farouk who had inspected them. According to my Granddad, the King had stopped and looked at him and said that he was doing a fine job. That was it, met the King of Egypt my arse. It was the same with his other story about being shot in the Pelopennese during the war. It wasn't till many years later I realised that the Pelopennese was a place in Greece and not a part of the body. Anyway, the goose was called Donald by my Gran, and Farouk by my Granddad and everybody that knew him. But, why should this be a mistake?

Well, as was said, the hens were kept for the eggs, but the intention had always been to fatten up the goose for Christmas, which was only a couple of months away, and when it arrived, did the issue of what to have for dinner cause trouble or what.

So, it's a few days before Christmas, and the goose is getting fat, as somebody once said. Expecting a good feed of goose and all the trimmings, quite a few of the family had decided to invite themselves for Christmas dinner. My Granddad didn't really want to part with his new found watch goose, neither did my Gran who had grown used to him. But, it was taking a lot of feeding, and there had been complaints about the honking at all times of the day and night. So, armed with a hatchet, my Granddad went round to the allotment to kill the goose. Or at least that's what he thought.

About five minutes after he left, there was a tremendous racket, and it was all coming from the allotment. Me and Gran went out on to the Pletty to have a look at what was going on. There didn't seem to be much sign of life, but given the noise, it was obvious quite a battle was going on. Then all of a sudden, we saw Granddad jumping up on to the billboards and throwing himself over into the street. A couple of minutes later he appeared on the Pletty. What a state he was in too. He was totally bedraggled, out of breath, had some marks on his head and hands where the goose had obviously pecked him, and he was covered in feathers. Round one to King Farouk.

Granddad realised that killing the goose wasn't going to be as easy as he thought. He went upstairs and enlisted the help of my two uncles, who having heard the racket had come out on to the top Pletty for a look. They too had seen the battle royal, and were a bit apprehensive about joining in.

At first, they had thought of using the slug guns, but Slaberee Alec was still a bit suspicious about the incident with Old Bert, so they decided against them. Besides, as Dode had said, it would take about a hundredweight of slugs to kill that big bastard. Anyway, ten minutes later, the three of then headed back round to the allotment. This time they were well prepared, or so they thought. As well as the hatchet, Grandad had a big fishing net, one of the ones with a pole and a hoop. Despite still sweating from the previous round, he had also put on his heavy overcoat as a sort of protection against the goose pecking him. My stepdad Eddie, had a hammer and had got a bin lid from round the backies. Uncle Dode though, was something to behold. He had dug out an old motorbike helmet from somewhere, along with a pair of goggles. He had also went round the backies and got a bin lid, and for a weapon he was carrying a long handled floor brush. It was like a scene from the 300 Spartans!.

So let battle commence. The three of them went into the allotment. The goose by this time really had its dander up, and the sight of the three of them sent it into a rage. It went charging at them flapping its huge wings and honking like a ships horn. The three of them suddenly took fright at this terrifying sight and run right back through the gate. A quick conflab, and they decided to split up and attack from three sides at once. Granddad would go through the gate, and when the goose charged, Dode and Eddie would go and climb over the billboards and take it from the side.

All went well, and as soon as Granddad appeared at the gate the goose went for him. Once it went to the gate, Dode and Eddie climbed over the billboards and got in behind the goose. They all charged at the goose who reacted by being even more noisy and aggressive.

The fall of the King of Egypt

They went at it for near twenty minutes, as one got Close the goose would go for him, and he'd back off. Then somebody else would try and he too would get repelled. Dode did manage to give it an almighty crack on the head with the brush, but the goose hardly even noticed. It was looking like goose was going to be off the Christmas menu. Then, help arrived in the form of Slaberee Alec.

By this time, the racket had attracted a few onlookers, some who were cheering for one side or the other. Slaberee Alec then came through the gate, went over to where the three of them had backed the goose into a corner between the hen house and the billboards, and asked what was going on. Granddad breathlessly told him about the Christmas dinner and what have you, and that they were trying to kill the goose. Is that all, Alec said, reached out a huge hand, grabbed the goose by the neck and pulled it toward him. Its easy enough, he said, and twisted the goose's neck right round a couple of times. The goose stopped flapping and hung there in his hands lifeless. Alec handed the now dead goose to Granddad and said to save him a bit, he was rather fond of goose he said.

The Mistake? Because the goose was given a name, it was looked on as more of a pet. So, despite all the carry on, it ended up that nobody would eat the bloody thing.

XXXII

So, there it was, New Year was here again. A great time to be an adult, not meant to be such a good time for bairns, but, given the history of Hogmany in the Rokie, that wasn't always the case. Something, usually something stupid, would happen to make it more memorable than it would otherwise have been. And this year was to be no exception.

Some of the more memorable new years, were like two years before when Dan Doogan set his hand on fire. Mind you, it was his false hand, and it was made of wood. That had all started innocently enough. The house was mobbed, everybody was well on with the drink and a sort of three and a halfsome reel was taking place to the usual sound of Jimmy Shand on the grammy. I said three and a halfsome reel, because the participants consisted of three people and Jimmy James, the midget pie man. He was so small that every time the dancers went to link arms for a birl, Jimmy's partner missed. The problem this particular time though, was that Jimmy's partner was Dan. As they both turned to link arms, Dan threw out his arm which went right over Jimmy's head. The momentum, plus the incredible amount of drink that Dan had drank, sent him flying towards the fireplace. As Dan went flying, he stood on an empty beer bottle and started to fall, instinctively putting out his hand, which went right into the fire. If it had been his real hand he would have reacted without thinking and pulled it out, but as it was his false hand and made of wood, he just took his time and used his hand to push himself up. When he did get up, his hand was on fire and blazing away merrily. Dan then done what I suppose anybody would do under the circumstances, he held up the hand to have a look, and said ***OH!***, then turned round to let everybody have a good look. He then went to the sink to run his hand under the well and near set the curtains on fire.

Then there was last year. Last year would eventually become memorable for all the right reasons, but it was still a bit of sore point, at least for some. Last Hogmany had started out in the same old way with everything being ready by around seven o clock as usual. The soup was made, the mashed tatties were in the pot, the steak pie was in the oven, and the sideboard was groaning under the weight of all the drink. Also as usual, we, the bairns, were expecting money to go to the show. Only problem was, nobody was around to provide us with the means.

The root of this problem seemed to lie with the fact that my uncle John was home from the navy, and as usual was doing his impersonation of Nelson, Rockefeller that is, not Horatio. At around five o clock, he had decided to take everybody, my Gran, Granddad, aunties, uncles, the lot, out for their tea at a place in the town. As we had been out playing in Foundry Lane, and didn't usually come back for show money till about seven, they decided they would have time, and so the lot of them took off. After they had finished eating at round half six, they started to head home. The male of the species intended however to have a few in the pubs in the town centre, while the women would head home. Problem was, that after the men had went into the first pub, the women had met up with one of my Grans cronies who told them she was going to a spookee meeting where some old wifey would be telling fortunes. It was starting at seven, so they went straight there, and we were forgotten about.

So, round about quarter to seven, the five of us arrived back at the Close and went straight to each of our houses to get show money. Samson and Delilah was on at the Royalty, and started around half seven. It took us about five minutes to realise that there was nobody around, and after a quick conflab we headed to Harry Bradleys, thinking that was where they would all be. I went into the boaly at Harry's, and Harry confirmed that there had been no sign of any of them, and that they had went into town for their tea. I thought that maybe Harry would bankroll us, and started to ask. Years of experience at dealing with moochers and skint drunks had taught Harry the impending signs of having the bite put on him. I opened my mouth and before a sound had come out a resounding **"No!"** had put the kibosh on that idea.

Nothing for it then, we headed back to my Grans house to wait. We sat impatiently in the house for what seemed an eternity, but in fact had only been about twenty minutes. But, it was getting near the show starting time, so we were very nervous. The show started in about fifteen minutes, and even taking into account Pearl and Dean and All Next Week, we would probably miss the start of the film. We had seen Samson and Delilah umpteen times before, but it was right at the start when there was a really great shot of Delilah in a see through dress. It was time for drastic action.

I suddenly remembered Granddad's empty beer bottle stash. He kept all his empties in the loabee press for when he was skint. There was generally a few there, and with my Uncle being home, there was bound to be extra. We dived into the press and there was a good couple of dozen empty screw tops, all worth thrupence each along at Harry Bradley's. We shared them out and ran like hell along to Harry's.

Cashing in the empties brought us seven bob on the nail. As it was one and a tanner each to get in, we didn't even have enough to go, let alone enough for as much as a choc ice between the lot of us. Then I remembered there was two and a half crates of screw top bottles of beer in the house for that night. A quick conflab and we headed back to Grans. Once there, we wasted no time and emptied the lot down the sink. Another dash back to Harry Bradley's brought us in another seven and a tanner, not only enough to get us all in, but enough for a choc ice and a Kiora each plus a couple of packets of Butterkist between us. Sounds great, but there would be a price to pay, and we all knew it.

I wont go into the detail of the rest of that new year, but I think its suffice to say that it involved us cowering in the back room and my Gran fighting of the male of the species with a poker. We might have got off with it, had it not been for Harry Bradley being at the house. When he heard about the beer, he had put two and two together, came up with five and squawked on us. Mind you, it was Harry agreeing to go back to the pub and get replacements that probably saved us.

This year however, was to be a completely new one. Something stupid would happen alright, and would become forever after known as: "The year wee Tam exploded".

For a change, everything had went smoothly that Hogmany, looking back, maybe too smoothly. We had got our usual show money, and the men had all came back from the pub at closing time, with Harry Bradley coming along an hour or so later. By midnight there was quite a turnout in the house, with all the usual suspects being there. Apart from the family there was Dan Doogan, Daft Tam, Jimmy James, Mick Feeney and Father Mahon. Just before midnight, everybody apart from Gran and Granddad, went out and came back in after the bells. The air was thick with the aroma of drink, fag smoke and goodwill. Jimmy Shand and Calum

Kennedy were giving it laldy from the grammy, and the floor was cleared for dancing. Soon the house was filled with heeoochs and the sound of feet thumping on the floor as the dancers gave it their all. By one, the party was in full swing.

Myself and the rest of the bairns had all been dumped together in the double bed in the back room, which also doubled as a cloakroom for the visitors. As more folk arrived, more coats were thrown on the top of us. This had been great fun for us, what with trying them on and doing impersonations of the owners and going through the pockets. By two, we were fed up with this, and decided to join in the party. We knew from experience that once they had all had a certain amount of drink, they didn't object to our gate crashing.

I opened the room door very slightly and had a look round at the festivities. The dancers were all knackered and had sat down to have a sing song. This meant having to endure all the individual favourites. Such as, Carolina Moonlight by uncle Chic, I Believe by uncle John, Blueberry Hill by auntie Marion, and of course, the murderous version of I Will take You Home Kathleen by Dan Doogan. There would be others, but the climax would always be When You Were Sweet Sixteen by Granddad, which would reduce my Gran and great auntie Belle to tears.

This was our cue, we were able to go through and sit with someone and be given our New Year, usually a glass of Cordial or Advocat and lemonade, although Dan Doogan and uncle John could always be depended on to give something stronger, like a drink of their beer, or a draw on a fag. This was to lead to this particular New Year being more memorable than usual.

My half brother, Thomas, aka, wee Tam, who by this time was three and a half, had been put in the room with us, but in the single bed usually used by myself. Remarkably, he had slept right through all the racket, both in the living room and all the capers we had been up to in the back room. Just as there was a lull in the sing song, wee Tam had come through dressed only in a vest with his bare arse and knob for all to see. He had a look round, saw us all sitting with a glass, and obviously wondered where his was. He spotted a glass of what he thought was lemonade of some sort, went over, picked it up and downed it one. Problem was, it was straight whisky, and not any old straight whisky either. It was some unbelievably bad shite that my uncle had brought back from America on one of his trips. It was called Davy Crockett's Pish or something, and it was so rough that even veteran whisky drinkers like Louie the Next and Dan Doogan had gagged on even a little sip of the stuff. There was a sudden silence, and everybody just sat opened mouthed at the sight of wee Tam downing this nip in a oner. Tam suddenly turned a strange colour, sort of greenish white, started to make strange faces, and his body was making funny twitches. What happened next had to be seen to believed.

The first to react was my uncle John, he grabbed Tam and picked him up, cradling his bare dowp on his arm with his face right up to his. Just as they came face to face, the nip started to have an effect on Tam's stomach, which reacted the only way it could. He turned pure white, then red, then blue and back to white again. Then, he just exploded.

By exploded, I mean various kinds of matter in an incredible variety of colours, came flying out at terrific speed from every orifice of his body. He puked, snottered, shit and pished himself all at the same time. Something I would never have believed possible. A torrent of puke and snotters came flying out his mouth and nose and hit uncle John right in the kisser. This was followed a split second later by another torrent, this time of watery skitters that flew out of Tam's arse all over my uncle's arm. Then to cap it all, Tam pissed all over my uncle's shirt. This wasn't the end though, far from it.

So, my uncle John was standing in the middle of the room with his face covered in puke and snotters, skitters dripping off his arm, and his shirt soaked with piss, and Tam still on his arm. Then to rub it in, Tam's face suddenly broke out in a big wide grin, and he let out a sighed **eeeeaaaaahhhhh.** Seconds later the silence in the room was broken as everybody gave a sigh of relief. Uncle John then held Tam out at arms length with the skitters still dripping off his backside and forming a pool on the floor. Uncle John asked if somebody would take him. My Mother suddenly awoke from what seemed like a trance, got up, took hold of Tam and held him also at arms length with the skitters still dripping off his dowp. Uncle John went over to the sink and rinsed his hands and arms under the well, washed the puke and snot off his face and dried himself with the dish towel. He gave out a loud ***Christs sake!*** and headed for the back room to change his shirt.

The year wee Tam exploded

My Mother, still holding Tam, looked round helplessly and pleadingly. Granddad was the first to react. He got up, took hold of Tam and took him over to the sink where he grabbed a cloth and wiped all the puke and snotters off his face. Then, turning on the cold well at full force, he turned Tam round and stuck his bare arse under the rushing water. Now, this was the middle of winter, and the water coming through this well was probably just above freezing point. That, and the fact that we lived at down at the docks, ie sea level, the force that the water was coming through was similar to that of a firies hose, which was more that enough to wash all the skitters of Tam's arse. But that was only part of it.

When the water hit his backside, Tam gave out a scream that would have curdled Boris Karloff's blood. Granddad gave Tam's arse a few seconds of this and turned the well off. He then took his cardigan that was hanging on the living room door, sat Tam down on the bunker, and put it on him. Granddad then took Tam over to my Mother and dumped him in her lap. **Right!** he said **whas turn fir i sang.**

XXXIII

When Luca was twelve and Gorgi only two, the first of a double tragedy was to devestate their young lives. Their father, Janos, who worked for the Gassy as a hole digging Executive, was killed. One day, he was working away in a particularly deep hole when there was an explosion. The explosion itself did not kill Janos, it was the earth round the hole caving in on him that caused his death. It was as simple and brutal as that. Janos had survived the war and a monumental trek across Europe, and died in a hole he had dug himself.

With the help of Tibor and his wife, Eszter did her best to bring up Luca and Gorgi on her own. It wasn't just a case of money, the Gassy had paid for the funeral and she got some compensation for Janos's death. She had always struggled to come to terms with life away from her homeland, and being there without Janos would be unbearable.

Eszter fell into a deep depression and spent most off her time in the house mourning her husband. She didn't look after the house or the boys, and for them it was often a case of food from the chip shop. Luca and Gorgi were good boys and never caused any bother, either at home or outside, and Tibor and his wife did their best to help Eszter. But he wasn't the only one who would take an interest in the boys welfare, or lack of it.

After the Tarzan in the jungle malarky in the Kirky, someone started to take an interest in the boys situation. Ezster received a couple of visits from such as the SSPCA, various welfare organisations and truancy officers. Nothing was done however, as apart from Ezster's depression, they could find no risk to the boys. The Truancy officer had been informed that there was a school age child in the house who had not been to school, but soon found that this meant Gorgi, who was still under school age. Luca was reported umpteen times to the police for incidents ranging from vandalism to fire-raising, but every time was found to have been somewhere else. From what Slaberee Alec was saying, all if it seemed to point to Cluny. But why?

Whether all of this became too much for Ezster is hard to say, but a year after her husband's death, she too died. Probably of a broken heart combined with all the stress and homesickness. By this time, Luca was fourteen and Gorgi was near five. They went to stay with their uncle Tibor who was also now on his own, his wife having died a couple of months previously.

It was round that time that Luca had started to draw snakes everywhere. Although there were all kinds of snakes, many of them resembled the ones his father had as tattoos. Then it happened, Luca drew a snake on Cluny's front door. This led to all sorts of mayhem, the Boabess got involved, Luca was charged and taken to the juvenile court. At the court both Luca and uncle Tibor were given warnings about future behaviour blah blah blah. For the next couple of years, Luca kept drawing snakes, but he stayed away from Cluny's house.

XXXIV

So, a Weelee Wag threw a hatchet at my uncle Dode.

One day, as usual, we were scutterin about in the Hutty. I fell over something in the long grass, and on investigating found that it was an old metal sign for cocoa. It was well rusted and faded, but it was obvious what it was. The Hutty had at one time been the ground on which a row of cottages had sat, and perhaps one of them had been a shop, or the sign had been up on the gable end of the end cottage. When I pulled the sign up, I also unearthed a load of other bits and pieces, probably left behind by the cottages owners. There was some bits of coal, a rusty shovel with a rotted wood handle, and a hatchet. It was one of those small hatchets that came with a set of other fireside tools: a poker, tongs and a brush. It was meant for chopping kindling, and was about nine inches long with a hollow metal handle. Despite being a bit rusty, it was in quite good condition.

I took the hatchet along to where the rest of the gang were and showed them it. I got a bit of stone and rubbed off the worst of the rust, then sharpened up the cutting edge on the Labour hall doorstep. Then taking shots each, we started to chop up every bit of wood in the Rokie. Nothing was exempt, washing poles, doorsteps, window sills, you name it. Then wee Dode had a flash of inspiration and said: ***mind that cowsir whar the Indian threw a tomahawk at a cowboy and it stuck in eez back.*** Remember it? You bet we did.

Less than half an hour later, we were round the backies. We got hold of an old door that had been lying about for ages, and propped it up against the wall next to the opening between the stairs and the Close. We had also drawn a cowboy on the door with chalk that some lassies had left lying about, probably for playing boxies. Then we started taking turns throwing the hatchet at the door. After about twenty shots each, where the hatchet had only stuck once, we began to suspect that the film was a load of shite. Then wee Dode took the hatchet, went right over to the Hutty wall, took a runny and threw the hatchet from about ten feet from the door. The hatchet went birling through the air, missed the door and clattered off the wall in a shower of sparks. It then went flying across the Close entrance at an angle, hit the opposite wall and bounced up the Close.

Problem was, just as the hatchet hit the wall in a shower of sparks, my uncle Dode, who had come down the stairs, walked past the opening between the stairs and the Close. The hatchet missed his head by about half an inch. Lucky for us, the hatchet bouncing away up the Close distracted him as he watched it and didn't look round to see where it had come from. This was our cue. We took off round the back of the stair turret, and looked round the edge of the boaly. We saw him coming back through the Close, hatchet in hand and going round the backies, obviously to find the hatchet thrower. As soon as he went out into the backies, we jumped up into the boaly, into the Close, out to the Lane, and run for it to Foundry Lane.

Later on, after we had all had our tea, we gathered round the backies as usual. The main topic was of course the hatchet throwing earlier on. Wee Dode and Ronnie said that their dad, my uncle Dode, had talked about it while they had their tea. He had asked where they had all been this afternoon, and they had said that they had been playing in the wood yard in Foundry Lane all day. It was a mystery then, he had said, somebody had thrown a wee hatchet at him, and when he went to look there was nobody around. He obviously hadn't put it together with the cowboy on the door. Wee Dode had then said: ***if it wiz i wee hatchet, mibee it wiz i Weelee Wag.***

Uncle Dode never did find out the identity of the mystery hatchet thrower. And far as I know, he went to the crematorium many years later, unsure of whether or not it was a Weelee Wag.

XXXV

It was round about the time that old Mrs Neep got her nickname, that Louie had another of these weird dreams.

Occasionally, people would appear round the backs of the tenements in the city. Musicians, singers and those selling stuff. One time, a man appeared carrying a set of bagpipes. He was obviously a Tink, and once round the backies, he started to play his pipes. However, he obviously didn't have a clue how to play them, and the racket he made was unbearable. This was probably his intention. I had seen him up on Princes Street outside a butchers shop one time. The butcher had come out and gave him a steak pie on condition he moved away. As he was droning away on his pipes, everybody in the land was out on their Plettys shouting at him to get lost. Next thing, the old wifey who live two doors along from us appeared and threw something at the piper. It bounced off the Tinks head, and on landing we could see it was a huge turnip. The Tinks pipes groaned to a stop, and he gave his head a shake and a rub. He then picked up the neep and left. I was never ever sure of what the old wifey's name actually was, but from then on she was known as Mrs Neep.

As usual, on the night he had the dream, Louie had been sitting in Harry Bradley's from opening to closing time. Around nine o clock, Obvious Joe had joined him at his usual table, and as usual stated the obvious about Louie reading the paper, which he was actually doing at the time. Joe was being an even bigger pain than he normally was and also asked if it was that day's paper. Although Louie would have loved to have said no, and that it was in fact last Wednesday's, he knew it would just lead to even more obvious and stupid questions from Joe, so he said that it was in fact that day's paper hoping that would be the end of it. It wasn't, and next thing Obvious Joe asks Louie what day it was. A simple enough request, and coming from anyone else Louie would have considered it a genuine thirst for knowledge. Before he got a chance to answer however, Pancake Tuesday, the Rokie know all, who was sitting at the next table, piped up that it was in fact United Nations day, the anniversary of the founding of the United nations organisation, and blah blah blah blah, blahed into a history of the UN. Louie was just about to tell him to shut his face and mind his own bloody business when the door opened and Sticky Tam walked in. Of all the things he could have said, it had to be ***Guess what day it is?*** Louie just put his head in his hands, sighed and waited for Pancake to kick off again, which he did, and again started on about the founding of the UN. Tam interrupted him and informed him no, it was more important than that. That really got Pancake going, 1857, the founding of Sheffield Wednesday, the worlds first football club. No, said Tam. 1929, the Wall Street crash, returned Pancake. Still no, and a lot more important, it should be etched forever in your memory, according to Tam. 1931, Al Capone got sent to Alcatraz. Again, a resounding no from Tam, followed with ***Its my bloody birthday, so where's my presents!***

Later that day, sitting at his sewing machine, Louie suddenly realised that there was in fact a particular significance to that particular day. One of the things that his old man had brought with him from the old country, was his customs and superstitions and important days and nights, and this just happened to be one of them, Martwynocny or something. It was some old Polish shite like Halloween here. The belief was, that on this particular night, if it was a leap year, from midnight to an hour before dawn, all the dead who had died violent deaths, from accidents, the murdered, the suicides, the executed, rose from their graves and walked in procession round the towns and villages, being joined by other victims as they passed their burial places. The belief was that only lunatics and the feeble minded could see the dead as they walked through the streets, so if you could see them, you too were a lunatic or feeble minded. So, to avoid any chance of seeing them, people would shutter and muffle up their doors and windows. On these nights, as Louie was growing up, his old man had shuttered the windows, closed the curtains and hung an old blanket over the top of them. He could remember these nights, lying in his bed as far under the covers as he could get, occasionally sneaking a look out and seeing his father sitting with the light out sewing away by the light from the fire. He had lost his fear as he got older, but always respected his dad's wishes to shutter and muffle up the window every leap year on Martwynocny.

That night when Louie got home after the pub shut, he went for a pee then before getting ready for his bed, he made sure the room window was well shut and the curtains closed up tight. Louie got undressed and into his pyjamas, gave the window and curtains one last check and got into bed. As he lay there trying to relax, memories of past nights such as these were in his mind, he could still see his father sitting sewing by the light from the fire and the feelings he himself felt as he lay in bed looking out through a slit in the covers. Before long though, as usual, Louie fell asleep, still thinking about Martwynocny.

At some time that night, Louie wasn't actually that sure when, he was wakened up by a clackety, clackety, clacking sound, like the sound a hundred people snapping their fingers all at once. He sat up in bed and looked round in the dark for the source of the sound, realising that it was in fact coming from outside. He rose from his bed and went over to the window, opened the curtains and leant forward to look out. What he saw made the hair on the back of his neck stand on end, he felt a chill go through his bones and his heart giving a lurch. The clacking sound was the noise coming from the bony feet of dozens of skeletons and decomposing bodies that were walking along the street outside. Clickety, clickety, clack, clack, clack, went the bones of the feet as they hit off the hard road stones beneath. The scene was lit up only by the green cast of the gas street lamps, which also cast long shadows of the dead as they walked along, adding to the eeriness of the scene.

Louie stood there, frozen stiff with fear. Then he saw a sight he wished he hadn't seen, there walking along in the parade was the newly dead Dan Doogan. As he passed, Dan turned and looked up at Louie. Then to make things even worse, standing leaning on a lamppost across the street, hands in pockets, was the idiot figure of Obvious Joe. He was standing there in a manner like he was watching an everyday event like a horse and cart go past. As Louie watched, Joe turned his head, smiled and nodded, as if to someone. Then Louie saw he was in fact reacting to something that someone had said, and that someone was daft Johnny who was walking along in the parade. Louie's fear heightened at this, it was not a fear of the dead outside, walking along in their hideous procession, but the fear of realising that he might be either a lunatic, or worse, a feeble minded idiot like daft Johnny or Obvious Joe.

Then, all of a sudden, he heard the high pitched wail of the siren at Halley's factory. He felt a sudden jolt go through him as he realised he was still in bed and the whole thing had been another dream. Louie got up from his bed and went through his usual morning rigmarole of tea, farts and fags. Sitting at the table, listening to the wireless, smoking his fifth fag and on his third cup of tea, he remembered and thought about the dream he had had. He remembered the sight of the dead Dan Doogan, the sight of the two idiots Obvious Joe and daft Johnny. Then, head resting on hand as usual, he muttered to himself ***Hope to fuck that was just a dream.***

XXXVI

In between the nood book shop and the pub, there was a Close which was the entrance to the flats above and out to the back of the building. The foot of the Close was the business premises of local entrepreneur, Lenny Black.

Lenny was a big man, tall and muscular, unlike so many men in those days. He was always well turned out, was clean shaved every day, and his dark, straight hair was always well groomed and styled without a hint of grease or Brylcreem holding it in place. He always wore a suit with a clean shirt every day, but never a tie, and his shoes were always well heeled and polished. Lenny was a good looking man, not a film star type like Johnny Athens, but there were many women in the Rokie who gave him long lingering looks as they passed by the Close.

Every day, except Sunday, no matter what the weather, Lenny would be standing there conducting business. This business consisted of taking bets on the horses, dogs, football, boxing, in fact anything. Lenny also lent money, but this was only to people who wanted money for betting. Lenny also had other business interests, but he only ran the bookies and money lending from the foot of the Close.

Basically, folk would go up to him and tell him what they wanted; two bob on some horse to win, a five bob treble or whatever. It didn't matter how complicated the bet: a five cross double, a yankee, a ten horse roll up, the gambler simply told him, never handed over the bet written on a bit of paper. It was the same when somebody won, they told Lenny their non de plume, and he handed over the winnings. The same applied to the money lending, the borrower said what they wanted, it was handed over, when it came time to pay it back, Lenny knew how much they owed. Nothing, absolutely nothing was ever written down. Or, so it seemed.

Black by name............

The money lending was not a business of Lenny's choosing. It wasn't a good idea to give credit to any would be gambler, but if they were skint, which most folk in the Rokie usually were, the bookies business suffered. So, the answer was to lend them money to pay the insurance man, the rent man or whatever, and if they chose to spend it on the horses, it was not his problem. Anyone who borrowed money, and Lenny never lent out more than a pound to anyone, paid back two bob for every pound and that was it. This was very reasonable, given the rates money lenders usually charged, but as he would often say, Lenny was not in the money lending business willingly. Defaulters, and there were very few, if any, simply had further credit ended till it was paid. There was never any question of enforcement, in fact the subject was never mentioned, even if Lenny and the defaulter happened to meet up. But, the defaulter would soon find that they not only couldn't get tick at the local shops, or in Harry Bradley's, they found that they couldn't buy anything, even if they had money. How Lenny had managed to arrange this with the shops and pub is a mystery, but he did. But then, shop and pub owners are practical people by and large, and knew that in a lot of cases, if Lenny didn't lend them the money, they themselves would have to give credit, so this way they all benefited. In most cases, the defaulter, faced with having to walk to another area, even for something as simple as a bottle of milk, or to go for a pint, usually paid up.

So, how did Lenny manage to run his paperless business? In a nutshell, he didn't. Basically, Lenny was just a bit smarter than the average bear, as someone once said. And certainly a lot smarter than the kind that went into illegal stuff like gambling and the like. His old man had been a street bookie and had done time in prison umpteen times, usually short stretches of thirty days or three months, which was the maximum. Most who were in that line of business accepted prison as an occupational hazard, some even as a break from the long hours spent on street corners in all weathers. It was, as Lenny said of his old man, part and parcel of the job. Lenny always wanted to follow his old man into the bookie business, but unlike his old man, only as a means to an end.

During his national service at the end of the war, Lenny, just like so many young men, was posted abroad. In his case, Lenny spent nearly two years in Italy and found there was more to life than bad weather, bad food, bad housing, bad jobs and subsistence wages. On coming home, his whole intention was to spend a few years getting enough money together through taking bets and a few other dodgy dealings, then retire to somewhere with decent weather, decent food and a decent place to live, in other words, anywhere but the shitehole he lived in. He also wanted to be young enough to enjoy this retirement, and so started young.

During his time in Italy, Lenny had got to know some of the local wide boys through his own dodgy dealings, especially in the thriving black market. One thing he did learn from them, was to always know the ins and outs of any law you intend to break on a regular basis. So, on coming home, the first thing he did was consult a lawyer about the ins and out of all the laws that he did intend to break ie. gambling, money lending and passing on of stolen goods. It turned out, that with gambling and money lending, it wasn't enough that money changed hands, there had to be hard evidence, in this case, betting slips or account books. So, Lenny realised, the obvious thing to do was not write anything down. He also realised that this wouldn't be as easy as it sounded though, given the amount of bets and money lent every day. He was no Marvo the Memory Man, the boy who had done a turn at the Broadway a while back, and even if he was, he would go on the stage himself. So, he had to find a way.

    Eventually, Lenny started taking bets and lending money from his pitch at the foot of the Close. Also eventually, the Boabees started taking an interest. The Boabees, in plain clothes, would stand further down the street and watch Lenny for hours on end. Folk would go up to him, tell him what they wanted, money exchanged hands, and that was it. At least a dozen times, the Boabees stepped in and took Lenny to the Boabees head office in Bell Street. They would search him thoroughly, but would only ever find money, and as Lenny would tell them, it wasn't illegal to be in possession of money. Neither was it illegal to take from, or give money to anybody. So the Boabees tried standing right next to him at the foot of the Close. On these occasions, folk wanting to do business with him, knowing from a great distance a Boabee in disguise trying not to look like a Boabee in disguise, just walked past. Although this was bad for business, the Boabees had nothing on him, and they knew it. Although they didn't give up entirely, apart from having a look now and again, the Boabees left him alone.

So how did Lenny solve the problem of never writing anything down. It was quite simple really. At the foot of the Close, right where Lenny stood every day, was a door. This door led to a stair that went down to the cellars under the building and also out to the rear. The cellars were for the use of the tennants, but as there was no light and a trip down meant a lot of scuttering around with torches or candles, they were very rarely, if ever, used. Lenny had got hold of a key to the door from somewhere or other, and had put it to good use. Just at the other side of the door there was a small landing, and on this landing, every day, same as Lenny, an old boy called Davy Thornton sat on a chair and wrote down every bet and loan that was transacted between Lenny and his customers. Lenny had drilled a whole load of tiny holes in the door right next to where Davy would sit, similar to what a priest listens to in holy confession. When the day's business was done, Davy would wait till Lenny gave the signal, then go down the stairs, out the back and go home to wait on the results. That night, when he had all the results, he would work out all the lines and who was due what. When the gambler came to collect their winnings the next day, he would whisper to Lenny the amount due through the holy door.

True to his word, Lenny did eventually go off to somewhere with better weather and food. Where exactly, nobody knew. Lenny just vanished one day around 1960. Whether he had decided he had enough for his plans, or whether he knew the game was up with betting, who knows. The Betting act had been passed that year, and legitimate bookies shops would be allowed to open from May the next year. Anyway, whatever it was, Lenny was never seen again, and the Rokie was a poorer place without him.

XXXVII

So, Daft Johhny got chased by a Cannibal.

One time, Sticky Tam asked Eck McLaren, the Coalman, for a shot of his lorry to go looking for wood up the coast and out in the sticks. Tinky McLaren and Frankie McPhee had asked if they could go along for the hurl, which meant that there was no room in the cab for Johnny. No bother to Johnny, the weather was ok and he enjoyed standing up on the back, leaning on the cab getting the wind in his hair and face. It was to turn out to be a memorable trip, but only for Johnny.

Anyway, after spending the whole day getting old tattie and fish boxes, along with a visit to some country pubs, they all headed back about seven o clock. Tam, a bit the worse for drink, took a bend too fast, and Johnny, who was standing on the back leaning on the cab, went flying off the back of the lorry and into a field. It happened so fast that Johnny didn't even get a chance to shout. So Tam and the lorry just went on as if nothing had happened.

What did happen, was like something out of a Charlie Chaplin film. Johnny went flying in an arc over the side of the lorry, over a dyke, landed on the grass, skidded on his front and went head first into a fence post. After the initial shock, it took Johnny a few seconds to realise what had happened. He pushed himself to his feet, rubbed his head and looking round, saw that he had just missed going face first into a massive pile of smouldering dung. ***Christ, that was lucky!*** he said out loud, looking at the pile of cows shite. Johnny jumped back over the dyke and looked up and down the road. He was still a bit stunned with his flight and crash landing and so had no idea what direction the lorry had been travelling in, or what direction it had come from. He also didn't have the faintest idea where he actually was. What direction should he go? Which way did the lorry go? Would they notice he was missing and come and find him? Johnny stood and thought about this for a couple of minutes, looking one way then the other up and down the road. There was only one thing for it ***eech meech hens keech toly bum fart*** he said out loud, while pointing in one direction then the other. On the word fart, he found himself pointing in the direction that the lorry had come from and away from where it had went. So, off he went, going god knows where.

Meanwhile a couple of miles down the road, Sticky Tam and the rest were oblivious to what had happened and were going like the bars to get back home before the pubs shut.

Half and hour later and a couple of miles up the road, Johnny realised it was starting to get dark. The road had been totally deserted since he set out, no people, no cars or lorries and not as much as a chink of light where there might be a house. Johnny kept walking, and as the light faded into darkness, he came to what appeared to be a huge stone standing up on end at the side of the road. He went over to the stone and standing beside it realised that it was even taller than him. It also appeared to be covered in signs and writing of some queer sort, and he reached out and touched it. Then he noticed there was a small sign on the dyke next to the stone. Even though the light was very dim, Johnny could make out some of the writing which was in big bold letters. As daft as he was, Johnny had learned enough reading at school to make out the words, and what he read sent shivers up his spine and the hair on the back of his neck and head began to rise. The sign said: **STANDING STONE. ERECTED BY THE PICTS CIRCA 600 TO 800 AD.**

On seeing the word Pict, Johnny started to remember the grisly tales told by Sticky Tam about the Picts. The Picts, according to Tam, didn't wear clothes and were covered in tattoos. Worst of all though, they didn't just kill their enemies when they caught them, oh no! nothing as simple as that, he had said. The Picts much preferred to take them back to their camps, and once there, skin them, roast them over a fire and then eat them. So, at the sight of the word **PICT,** Johnny just turned and ran as fast as he could, looking back as if the stone would suddenly come to life and chase him.

A few minutes later, Johnny realised neither the stone or anything else was chasing him, so he stopped and sat down on the grass verge to get his breath back. After a few minutes, he got up, looked round to check if there were any Picts about, then seeing it was all clear, started off down the road again.

Johnny walked on for another half an hour or so until it was near total darkness. There was a bit of a moon, which gave some light, but really just added to the sense of eeriness. At every little sound or movement, Johnny's heart would give a jump and he would walk a little faster. Then, in the distance, he saw a light. He hurried his pace at the sight of this, and within a couple of minutes he found himself in front of a cottage. He had a good look at the little cottage which had a garden in front and a gate through which there was a path leading to the door. Above the door there was a light, which must have been the one he had seen from the distance. Should he knock? What would he say? Would they have any ice lollies? Would they just tell him to bugger off? It had been some time since he had had anything to eat or drink, and by now he was really hungry and thirsty. Eventually he plucked up the courage and opened the gate, went up the path and knocked at the door.

Daft Johnny's pictish adventure

After knocking a couple of times, Johnny heard movement inside the cottage, and then slowly, the door opened. There standing in the doorway was a man, a big man, much bigger than Johnny, but obviously quite old. He had grey hair and despite being well built, was slightly stooped and had a walking stick. He had on a pair of cord breeks, a sark with armbands and the biggest pair of tackety boots that Johnny had ever seen. The man asked Johnny in what Johnny described later as a choochter accent, what he could do for him. Johnny started to stammer out what had happened, leaving out the bits about the standing stone and of course about the Picts. It took some time, but eventually the old man got the gist of the story and told Johnny to come in.

Johnny followed the old boy into what he took to be the living room of the cottage. There was no light on, but there was a fire burning away in the fireplace. The old lad asked Johnny to sit down on a chair at one side of the fireplace, while he sat on a chair at the other side. They both sat and looked at each other in the orange glow of the firelight. The man told Johnny in his choochter way that the only way back to the city was to get a bus from the village a couple of miles away, but that he didn't think there would be one by the time he got there.

The old man had realised pretty early on that Johnny was a couple of neeps short of a field, and that he would have to do something to help him. The old man told Johnny, that late as it was, he had a car and would give him a lift back home, to which Johnny gratefully nodded. The old boy then said that he was still in his working clothes, and if he just waited a couple of minutes he would go and get changed.

The old boy then left the room and Johnny had a look round. The room was very clean, and had some nice furniture and bits and pieces, more like what a wifey would have, Johnny later told Tam, but there wasn't a wifey there. A few minutes later, the door opened and the old boy came in. He had on a pair of good breeks, shoes, and as he was carrying a white sark, nothing else. At this Johnny again felt the chills in his spine and his heart starting to race like an express train. The old man had tattoos all up his arms and a huge one on his chest. *A PICT!* Was what went screaming through Johnny's head, *A*

BLOODY PICT! Then the old man said: ***Right, now for something to eat.***

The sight of the tattoos was bad enough, but at the sound of the old boy saying something to eat, Johnny let out a shout, got up, barged past the old man and pulled the door open. He run into the lobby of the cottage, pulled the front door near of its hinges and run out into the night. Johnny run down the garden path and louped over the gate like an Olympic hurdler. His momentum was so great he run right across the road and into the dyke on the other side. Johnny obviously hurt himself when he banged into the dyke, but he never even noticed. By that point he was a man possessed with only the intention of getting away as far as he could from the cottage. Johnny just ran and ran and ran in the darkness with his fear driving him on. If someone from the Olympic selectors had been timing him, Johnny would have been in the team for the next games no bother.

It was only when Sticky Tam and the rest of them arrived back at the yard that they realised Johnny was missing. Tinky and Frankie were for just going to the pub for the last hour. But Tam realised that if Johnny had fallen off the lorry and wasn't hurt, he wasn't the kind to be able to find his way back. There was nothing else for it but to go back and look for him. Tam turned the lorry round, he went back to Eck's yard and put some fuel in the tank, then headed back the way he had came.

It was near four in the morning when they eventually found Johnny sitting in a wooden bus shelter a few miles from where he had fallen off the lorry. It wasn't till the next day however, that Tam managed to get the story of the Cannibal out of a now not so terrified Johnny. After hearing all the details, Tam just said to Johnny: ***well, it kidda been worse, yi might i landed in that pile i shite.***

XXXVIII

As much of an idiot that Obvious Joe was, eventually he did manage to get a part time job.

It all came about when one of Joe's mum's neighbours managed to get Joe a job. It didn't last long though, in fact he started at midnight and got sacked at a minute past. He was actually there for around six hours, but it was back dated by five hours and fifty nine minutes.

The neighbour worked in one of the bakeries just outside the Rokie. It was obvious that the manager who had agreed to give Joe a job didn't live locally, or he would never have let him over the door. The job was actually quite simple, putting the fillings in the pies and tarts. Well, simple enough for most folk, but the manager and the neighbour had seriously overestimated Joe's abilities.

To make pies and tarts, the Bakery had a machine that made the casings and tops. The casings were all the same, but the tops were different, with the tart tops being rippled round the edges. Joe's job was to take a tray of casings, put in a scoop of filling, then put the tops on. They would then be taken to the ovens, baked, then be taken in vans out to the shops. So, there it was.

Joe was shown by the neighbour how the filling worked. There was a bowl of minced mutton for the pies, and bowl of cooked apple for the tarts. This was just too complicated for Joe. When the mutton run out, he just used the apple, when another bowl of mutton was put on his bench, he just used that. Then when it came to the tops, he just couldn't remember what was what and just put them on as they came. When he was done, the whole lot, 600 pies and 600 tarts, were taken away to the ovens. The baker simply stuck them in the oven, gave them the specified time, took them out and put the trays over to where the vanmen put them in the vans. The vanmen were a bit annoyed that the pies and tarts were all on the same trays together, but apart from that nobody noticed there was a slight problem. Next day however, was a different story..

From the minute they opened the following day, the owners of the various shops that the Bakery supplied were inundated with complaints, and even a couple of compliments. All the complaints concerned the previous day's pies and tarts, and were along the lines of: ***Aipil tert wi beans! Wha ir yi trehin ti kid!*** And ***Broon sas on in aipil tert!*** Or ***mutton peh n custard, ir yi trehin ti piysin iz!*** One boy though, said that brown sauce on his apple tart was quite nice.

Meanwhile, unaware of this, Joe was back that day filling pies and tarts. Once he became aware of the situation, the manager heaved Joe out of the Bakery, telling him that any money he was due would go to paying back the customers. So, that became Joe's first, last and only ever job.

XXXIV

The night before I developed a fear of midgets, I had been up all night with a serious dose of the skitters. Umpteen times, my Granddad had to take me out to the lavee. Normally, during the day, I would have went on my own, but my Gran told my Granddad that as it was the middle of the night, he had to take me. He wasn't too chuffed about this and let me know as much. Mind you, if it had been left to him, he would have just sat me on the sink.

On one of the numerous trips, as we walked along the Pletty in the dark at god knows what time of the morning, we saw a couple of figures walking along Blackscroft. Simply due to the difference in size between the two of them, I recognized the figures as big Jim Anderson and wee Sammy Dodds. They also each appeared to be carrying something, and were keeping exceptionally quiet. My Granddad also spotted them and said that the water board must have found a leak somewhere. I was a bit baffled by this, and when I questioned him, Granddad just said he would tell me some other time..

So, what was that all about? Big Jim and wee Sammy were aptly named. Big Jim was around six foot two, and built like the proverbial shithouse. Sammy on the other hand, was about four foot ten and of average build. Although only Sammy lived in the Rokie on Blackscroft, they were often seen together doing their work with the water board. Jim and Sammy had worked together for the water board for some forty odd years. They had both started work together as labourers after leaving school. At first, they worked on the big jobs doing all the menial stuff like making the tea and going messages. As they got older they were put on more important jobs, like digging trenches. For the last twenty odd years, they had worked as a pair. Their job was to go in to the depot in the morning, and then be directed to where there was a leak. They would then take a hand cart with all the necessary gear and go to where they had been directed. When they got there, they would dig till the leaking pipe was exposed, wait till it was repaired, then fill in the hole again. If the men who done the repairs couldn't get there that day, they would erect barriers and leave lamps beside the hole. Simple as that.

So, why were they out in the middle of the night? The story I eventually got, was that five years earler, they had been sent to dig a hole in Baffin Street, just outside the Rokie. The hole they dug was to repair a leak in a pipe that supplied a tenement. The tenement in question was next door to a pub. It had been a particularly hot day, and the owner of the pub, who knew them, came out and asked if they fancied a pint. They both said no, as drinking during working hours wasn't allowed. The owner then said that a shandy wouldn't do any harm, and told them to come in. Ten minutes later, one of the gaffers of the board turned up, and found that they weren't there. He went in to the pub and found them standing at the bar, pint glasses in hand.

The upshot of it all was that Jim and Sammy lost their jobs. They tried everything to get back to work, but for whatever reason, the board wouldn't back down. So, from then on, every time the water board dug a hole in the area, Jim and Sammy would go to it during the night and fill it in, barriers, brazier, tools, lamps the lot. They even dug the hole a bit deeper one time, so they could bury the hand cart as well. One time, when the board had dug a thirty foot long trench to put new pipes down in Ferry Road, Jim and Sammy had enlisted the help of some volunteers, including Sticky Tam who thought it would be a good laugh.

The whole malarky had cost the water board dear over the years. They had to employ watchmen on a near twenty four hour basis, and then had the extra cost of re-digging the holes. Some time later, the whole thing just stopped. Nobody knew why Jim and Sammy had ended their vendetta against the water board, and they themselves weren't saying, and never did.

XXXV

Occasionally, conflicts would arise between bairns from different areas. If a crowd came down from another area and tried to take over your patch, or if a new patch became vacant, it would have to be decided whose it was. Negotiations were non existent, the only solution was war. For bairns at the time there were many weapons available for times of conflict. However, of these weapons, there was one that was considered the most deadly. If the Geneva Convention knew about it, it would be on the list of banned weapons. This weapon was the **Dubit.** The Dubit was a fiendish weapon. Being hit meant muck in your hair, down your sark, in your shoes, and the prospect of what you got when you went home in this state.

The Dubit could be used in a couple of ways. The best was to drop it on an unsuspecting victim right on top of the napper. This way the victim got the full effect, hair covered in muck with the surplus penetrating right down all sides of the sark. One of our favourites was to wait at the back railings of the swing park. The swing park was on the roof of the Foundry in Foundry Lane, and so there was a drop of about 40 feet. When a suitable victim came along, we would drop the Dubit on them, not always successfully. If the victim decided to give chase, it meant a climb up some four sets of stairs. By then, we were long gone.

One time, after going to see The Dam Busters, we decided to work it all out as to how to use a dropped Dubit to best effect. We stood at the railing at the swings, and using stones dropped on to a drain cover on the pavement below, worked out exactly when to drop the Dubit on to a victim. We got hold of some Dubits then lay in wait. Eventually, a couple of men came along. They were what was known as Coolies, off one of the ships that had come to the city with a cargo of Jute. The two of them were walking side by side, something we hadn't put into our calculations. The Dubit was dropped, and right enough it was bang on target, **if** someone had been walking along on their own in the middle of the pavement. The result was that the Dubit went right between the two men's heads and landed on the shoulders of one of them. Before they got a chance to look up, we had scarpered, laughing our heads off, out the swing park, across the road and round to Constable Street. This wasn't the end of it though. Next day, we were lying in wait again. Next thing I know is, a hand with dark skin has got hold of my right wrist. This is the hand that I'm holding the Dubit in. Then I was birled around face to face with the two men from the day before, the men we had dropped the Dubit on. My half brother and cousins instantly took off at this point. Next thing I know, the man who had grabbed my wrist, takes the Dubit and hits me over the head with it. ***Laugh now*** he said, ***go on, you laugh***. Needless to say, I didn't.

Mainly though, the Dubit was thrown. The best type of Dubit for this, was one pulled out of long grass, that way it could be swung around a couple of times before being thrown. The most effective use of the thrown Dubit, was to throw en masse. Twenty or thirty Dubits flying at the enemy at one time, was usually enough for a retreat. Occasionally though, both sides had the same idea.

One such time, a conflict took place that became known as the battle of Halley's Brae. Forget Culloden, forget Waterloo, they were mere punch ups compared to Halley's Brae. Wallace Street, that ran between Blackscroft and Princes Street, was always called Halley's Brae for obvious reasons; on either side of the street was Halley's mill and warehouses.

It all started after some workmen turned up and demolished one of the small storage sheds at the corner of Constable street and Halley's Brae. A few days later, a couple of lorries dumped a load of building materials on the ground where the shed had been. There were bricks, timber, and a huge pile of sand. To us, this was like super santa had turned up and left a massive pile of toys. Not just us, but all the bairns from Foundry Lane turned up and started to build various structures. laddies built forts and castles, while wee lassies built houses for their dollies. We didn't usually get on with the Foundry Lane lot, but this was too good a fun to mess up with arguments about who had what. We played there all the first day till it was near dark, and even then we had to be physically dragged home. Still, we thought, there was always tomorrow.

This was when the trouble started. Next day, we headed up to the building plot, and resumed where we had left off the night before. An hour or so later, I heard an almighty thud against the side of the fort we had built. I stuck my head up and looked out. There they were, a whole gang, about twenty of them, had come down from Wallacetown, an area just the other side of Princes Street. One of them, obviously the leader, said that the building site was theirs, and so we better get lost. He had a stone in his hand, and next thing he threw it in my direction. He obviously never intended to hit me, as like me, he knew the damage a stone can do. I told wee Dode to go to the side of the plot and get me a Dubit, which he did. I told the lot of them in no uncertain terms to bugger of, and threw the Dubit. It too missed, but on hitting the wall behind them, it splattered muck all over the whole gang. ***Right!*** Said the leader, ***Yiv ast fir it, we'll be back!***

Time for action. I shouted to everybody to get together as many Dubits as they could get. Everybody started to gather together all the Dubits they could from around the edges of the site where their was long grass. There wasn't that many, the site had been cleared and there was no other open spaces where Dubits grew. So, time for drastic action. We all got together and after a conflab, run back down to the Rokie. Everything and anything that could be used to carry Dubits was purloined. Piles of Dubits began to appear at the site in bin lids, bread boards, trays, even the wee lassies had put their dollies aside and had filled the prams with them. Less that fifteen minutes later, we had enough ammo to fight off an army.

Fifteen minutes after we had got back to the site, the Wallactown mob turned up. They too had been busy, and had masses of Dubits too. Then let battle commence. The air was so full of flying Dubits, that they nearly blotted out the sun. Thrown Dubits were picked up and thrown back, and occasionally somebody from one side or the other, would make a run forward and throw a Dubit from point blank range. One of the Wallacetown lot did, and before he knew it, got pelted by about twenty odd of them himself. We had the advantage of being on the defensive, and so inside our forts. This also meant though, that if a Dubit landed inside, it made a hell of a mess. The battle went on for some minutes, and eventually the ammo run out on both sides. The Wallacetown lot stood back and shouted all sorts of insults which we shouted back, then they scarpered. We thought we had won the day, but didn't realise that right behind us stood the figure of Slaberee Alec. We just suddenly heard the words, **ok ok what the hells this a aboot?**

That was the end of that **ald sang.** I looked down at myself, I was covered in muck from head to foot, I felt in my hair, it had muck right to the scalp. I pulled my shirt out and a whole load of muck and worms fell to the ground. I looked round at the rest, and they were just as bad, we looked like the Black and White Minstrel Show. I took off my shoes and about half of Scotland fell out on to the ground. Then I realized Slaberee Alec was trying to keep his laugh in. **So,** he says, **whit was that a aboot.** I told him the story of the takeover bid by the Wallacetown lot. **Well**, he said, **um gled yi think it wis worth it, cos the men start work the morn, and thill be a wahtchy here a the time.**

So, despite all our efforts and acts of valour, this was the last time we'd be playing with the building stuff. Realizing that as soon as we got home, my mother, aunties and my Gran would be out with the zinc baths, the carbolic and the dreaded scrubbing brushes, we decided to stay and make the best of it.

XXXVI

So there we were, back with the Haidee again. We never found out what happened to Miss Clarke, even whether she stayed in teaching. Maybe she decided on an easy life, and took a job in the prison service or something.

For two solid days we had to endure the Haidee's idea of primary education. Reading lessons comprised reading aloud long parts of the bible or other holy wullie stuff, sums usually meant counting up something to do with church collections on Sunday, while even handwork meant making a bible cover or whatever. That is, when we managed to fit some work in at all. As soon as we got in the class in the morning, we had to have a prayer and a bible lesson. By the time the Haidee was finished it was playtime, or time for milk, which usually meant a thank you for the milk prayer.

A couple of days later however, we went into the class first thing to find someone sitting at the teacher's desk. This person, I wont say woman, cos at this point, none of us were that sure whether it was male or female, told us to sit down and ***BE QUIET!!!!!*** With a serious emphasis on the be quiet bit. We all sat down, and "<u>Miss</u>" Ferguson introduced herself. She told us how we had fallen behind in our schooling through having to change teachers so much, but she would make sure we would soon catch up. This was all said in a tone of voice that indicated that it was really us who were at fault, and any nonsense would be severely dealt with. We were all sitting there in silence, not because we were listening, but because we were trying to figure out what she was. She had the regulation short cropped hair with no attempt at styling, and was wearing what I took to be a blue shirt buttoned up to the neck. But, nothing could have prepared us for the sight that appeared when she stood up and walked over to the blackboard. The top half of her body was quite slim and she appeared to have no breasts at all. The lower half however, was mind boggling. What appeared to be a slim mans body, seemed to be sitting on top of the most enormous waist, arse and legs imaginable. She was dressed in a skirt that went down to her elephant size calves, while her enormous feet were encased in a pair of huge sandals and ankle socks. She looked for all the world like an enormous five year old. It was like two different people had been sewn together at the waist. At playtime, we talked about her, and reckoned she must have been part of a magic act where two people get sawn in half and put together again, only the two halves had got mixed up.

    Miss Ferguson was as good as her word about getting us to catch up. For the first couple of weeks, she had us going at it hammer and tong. It was all three Rs stuff, and no handwork, art or stories. She had managed to keep us at it, not because she was any good as a teacher, but through the threat to send us along to Clarky. Clarky was the deputy headmaster, and a complete cunt. He had a belt that he had obviously hardened with Surgical Spirit, an old sadists trick, and had no qualms about laying it on multiple times, even to the youngest of bairns. He too eventually left the school after getting a belt in the pus from the irate parent of a six year old. Unlike Clarky though, it wasn't the belt that was to lead to Miss Ferguson's departure.

    One afternoon, she had us doing sums as a class. This entailed her standing at the blackboard, writing out a sum, and calling out one of us to do it. This went on for a while, then she called up one of the boys, Pete Chalmers. Pete went out and stood at the board as told, she gave him the chalk and told him to write the answer. As he was standing there scratching his head totally baffled, she had the box of chalk in her hand, trying to sort it all out by colour. Inadvertently, she dropped the box and crouched down to gather it up. As she was crouched down, her long skirt spread out over the floor. It just had to happen, without realising, Pete moved his foot and stood on the skirt. When Miss Ferguson stood up, the skirt stayed down. So, when she was fully upright, the skirt was round her ankles, and we all got an eyeful of her huge backside encased in the biggest pair of flowery knickers we had ever seen.

Her reaction to this was, I suppose, not unexpected. She reached out her hand and pushed Pete away. It was probably the unexpectedness, but she used a lot of force and Pete went flying. He went sideways, staggering and reeling and crashed right into a radiator. Miss Ferguson then grabbed her skirt, and started to pull it back up while running towards the door. She disappeared out the door, and left us all sitting there in shocked silence. It took a couple of minutes for us to get over the initial shock, but then we all started to laugh and talk about those enormous knickers.

The Haidee must have been busy or something, because a few minutes later, his secretary appeared and stayed with us for the rest of the afternoon. She just dished out some books and left us to it, but best of all, the secretary was an absolute doll. Again, that was the last we saw of Miss Ferguson.

XXXVII

Plenty of articles have been written about the street games that bairns used to play, games that appear to no longer exist, games which were generally harmless to both the bairns and the local populace. In every town there were versions of hide and seek, games with balls, games meant to annoy people by doing things like knocking at doors and running away. (This is now called Parcel Force). I played all of these games as a boy, but there were also a few that nobody has ever written any twee stories about. There were also games that showed the darker side of the nature of the participant, revenge.

One such variation involved pushing a safety pin into the putty of a window frame in such a way as to be very difficult to detect. A roll of thread or thin fishing line was attached to the pin which was then let out to the perpetrator's hiding place. The perpetrator would then give a slight tug on the line making the safety pin ping against the window. The occupant would come to investigate, but of course would see nothing. This annoying carry on could go on for some time, till either the perpetrator got fed up or the victim came out to investigate further and found the pin. This irritating game was usually carried out at random, or simply because the victim had all the suitable elements of a convenient window and hiding place. But, it was also reserved as a means of payback on those who wallowed in giving youngsters a hard time.

One such was Eb Watson. Eb, of course, wasn't his real name, we just called him that after Ebeneezer Scrooge. Eb moved into one of the ground floor houses in our tenement when I was about eight. On the ground floor there were three houses, two that were accessed from the Close, and one that had its front door on the street. Eb moved into the house with its door on the street.

Eb was without a doubt the biggest greeting face old git that ever lived on the planet, and if they ever find life on other planets, I bet they wont find a bigger greeting face there either. It was just the usual old "I hate everybody, but especially bairns" sort of stuff. Keep off the shelters, keep out of his back green, stop standing outside his window, stop playing there, keep away from his door, go and play at your own door, stop breathing, stop existing, stop being a bairn, etc. He was so bad, that even other greeting faces, and there were plenty around our area, called him a greeting face old git, and never felt the slightest bit sorry for him, no matter what we did to him.

The first time we did the pin in the window trick to Eb was a sight to behold. So much so that when we told Sandy Thom, an elderly neighbour about it, he laughed so much he nearly choked on his fahlsers, and gave us a half crown to share between us. Eb lived on the ground floor, and as usual when it got dark about seven o clock, we sneaked up and stuck the pin in the window frame, rolled out the thread to our hiding place among the bins and started to ping his window. It took a few seconds, but eventually Eb appeared at the window, bonnet on as usual. He wore his bonnet all the time, even in the house. We once saw him standing at his window having a shave with his bonnet on. When he appeared at the window, his head just came through the curtains, he took a casual look around, then pulled his head back in. We waited a couple of minutes then gave another ping on the glass. Again, a few seconds later, his head came through the curtains, and this time he had a good look round. We done this a few times till eventually Eb pulled the curtains open and came right up to the window for a serious look around and then came out into the dark back green. Eventually, he went back in. We waited a minute or so, then gave a tug, only this time Ebs head suddenly rose up from under the sill and appeared at the window. He must have crawled up to the window and waited on the ping then jumped up suddenly hoping to see what was the cause of the sound. We laughed so much that we nearly gave our hideout away. The thought of him crawling along on all fours to below the level of the window sill and then suddenly jumping up was too much for us. We didn't want to spoil a good thing, and besides it was something we wanted to share with others, so we waited a while and rolled the thread in and retrieved the pin for another night.

    One of our favourites, and not one always reserved for mortal enemies such as girners, involved finding matches, a newspaper and a lump of dogs shite. First you find a good size lump of dog shite, preferably newly laid, not a problem around these parts in them days. Once you have a suitable shite, you go to the victims door and place the shite on the doorstep, tear off a piece of the newspaper and place it over the shite, then light the paper, knock at the door and run. The object was, that the victim would then come to the door, see the burning paper and stamp it out with their foot which would then get shite all over the sole. This was particularly effective if the victim was wearing slippers, only socks, or even better, but rare, bare feet. Although never seen, there was also the thought of the victim having to hop back up their lobby to the sink to get cleaned up. When we done it to Eb, we were hiding just outside the Close, so could hear his foot stamping as he hopped back up his lobby screaming what he was going to do to us. Another elderly neighbour, old Mrs Hickey, bought us all a slider each for that one. This was not usually a random trick though, or carried out very often, as once done the victim never got caught again, So it was generally reserved for real swines like Eb.

There was also another version of this which involved a bin raking expedition to find a big empty tin, something like a family size soup or bean tin. Once a suitable receptacle was found, we would approach the victims Close, then we would all take a turn at pishing into the tin. The tin was then placed at an angle against the foot of the victims door, which took a careful hand and some patience to accomplish and quite often ended with the doorstep soaked in pee. Once the tin was balanced, the door was knocked at and we would scarper. The victim would come to the door, open it, the tin would overbalance and the contents would flood into the **loabee.** This was a trick that could be carried out repeatedly on the same victim as they had no idea what was outside the door till they opened it, but it was again usually reserved for mortal enemies like Eb.

One time, Eb really pushed us to the limit. This time, so bad that we all cut our hands with a razor blade and swore a blood oath of revenge against him. ***Death To the Tyrant*** was our oath. My uncle John, home from the navy, came out one day when we were kicking a ball about at the junction of Foundry Lane and Peep o' Day Lane. He joined in our game of shootie in, and it showed that he really fancied himself as a centre forward, as every cross had to be to his head. The ball we were using was just a small plastic effort that we had found along at the grassy beach one time. Uncle John decided we should have a real tub, and took us up to a shop on Princes Street where he bought one. it wasn't a full size or weight tub, but to us, it was like playing at Hampden in a cup final. Every time we used it, it would be cleaned and put away somewhere safe, instead of the usual of just leaving it lying in the street.

It had to happen though. Playing one day down at the junction, Eb suddenly appeared from along Foundry Lane. We were nowhere near his or any other house, in fact there wasn't a window or anything breakable in sight. Still, Eb grabbed the ball and took it with him up to his house. He went in, came back out again with a knife, and right in front of us, stuck the knife in to the tub. He then dropped the tub on the pavement and went back in. My uncle John by this time was away back to sea, and words to Eb from my Gran and Granddad fell on deaf ears. Not that we were bothered though, we had plans of our own for Eb. But what?

One day, my Granddad told us that there was a ship in the dry dock. Over the next few days, the water would be pumped out leaving the ship shored up with timber. This meant, according to Granddad, that there would be dozens, if not hundreds of crabs and eels lying in the bottom of the dry dock. Granddad loved cooked eels and crabs, and he told us about how he intended to get a bucketful, and have a feast. But after thinking about this, an idea started to form in my mind.

The next day, me and the gang went over to Halleys and scrounged an old jute sack off one of the workmen sitting out the back at dinnertime. When Granddad came home to tell us that the dry dock was now empty, we went down and gingerly picked up a few eels and crabs and put them in the sack. When we got back to the Close, we went round to the backies, where we found Ebs bedroom window slightly open. It took a bit of careful effort, but we managed to put the whole lot through the gap and into his bedroom.

Later that night, me and Granddad were sitting watching Gunsmoke on the TV. Even over the noise coming from the set, we could hear Eb giving it laldy. I sat and had a little grin to myself, trying to picture Eb jumping around his bedroom trying to avoid the eels and crabs. A few minutes later, there was a thunderous knock at the door.

Gran, who was standing at the sink washing some clothes, went to answer it. Next thing, there is the sound of a huge argument out on the Pletty. Me and Granddad run to the door just in time to see Gran planting a right cross on Ebs face. My Gran was wee, but boy was she tough, and that punch was worthy of Sugar Ray himself.

The upshot of this was that we got a visit from Slaberee Alec, who Eb had went girning to after his belt in the pus. While eating a huge plate of peeces courtesy of Gran, Alec told us that Eb now had a huge keeker. He also said that Eb had managed to round up all the eels and crabs, but that his house was now reeking of fish. Seemingly, Eb had wanted to press charges against Gran, but Alec had talked him out of it, saying that maybe it wouldn't look good in the paper that he'd got that black eye from a woman.

A couple of weeks later, Eb moved out of the house. Seemingly he had moved to a brand new house in one of the schemes. One of the houses meant for elderly folk, in a Close with just other folk his own age. That, I imagine would be hell on earth for Eb. No bairns to girn at.

XXXVIII

A couple of days after Wee Tam became the only cowboy with a kilt, Louie had the third and weirdest of his weird dreams.

We were all dressed up again, one of my cousins was getting married, and we were all invited, bairns an all. I don't know what possessed

Have kilt - will travel

my mother, but one day up in Menzies, she got talked into buying a complete Highland outfit for Tam. It had the lot, kilt, jacket, tie, socks and shoes. He looked like a miniature Andy Stewart. Problem was though, that once she got him dressed up in this get up, he refused to go out without his cowboy guns and hat. This was a sight to behold, a full Highland outfit, plus a belt with two holsters, guns and a cowboy hat. It just had to end in tears though.

My mother, auntie and Gran told us all to go out and play till it was time to go to the Kirk. This was accompanied by a warning to keep clean. However, just at the top of the lane, some men were repairing the road, and had a tar boiler on the go. We watched as the men turned the tap on the boiler to fill a bucket with tar, then mix it with gravel. Tam went over to the tap as it was flowing, stuck his gun under the flowing tar which performed an arc and splattered him from head to foot. Needless to say, Tam and my stepdad weren't at the wedding. The staff at Maryfield did get something to talk about though, when a tar covered cowboy in a kilt walked in to casualty.

As usual, Louie had been drinking from opening till closing in Harry Bradley's, and had managed to drag himself out the pub by 10 o clock. Sticky Tam and Tinky McLaren were still there, and being involved in a game of dominoes with Harry, looked like they were there for a night of it. Louie had actually been glad to get away from the pub that night. The hanging of a man convicted of a particularly nasty murder was due to take place the next morning, and so the papers and the wireless news were full of particularly vociferous arguments for and against the death penalty. The pub had been no different that night, and those for and against had been giving it more that the usual laldy. Like Sticky Tam's comment that hanging was in fact too good for this boy that was about to be hung, and in fact a good kick in the arse was what he needed. Of course things were made all the worse by the likes of Obvious Joe asking if it was sore getting hung, and by Pancake Tuesday and his who got hung when. Even Tinky McLaren, who was generally a quiet type, was more vocal then usual in his protests against hanging. But this just gave Sticky Tam a good opportunity to wind him up and make things worse, which was actually his whole intention. He started going on about how Tinky was just against it cos he was a Tinky, and that more Tinkys had been hung than murderers in the last couple of hundred years. In fact in the old days a Tinky was hung just for being a Tinky, if folk saw a Tinky they just went and got a rope and took him to the nearest tree. Which, according to Sticky Tam, was the reason there were no trees in the highlands, as the Tinkys had cut them all down in a fly move to get the hanging of Tinkys stopped. And did Tinky McLaren know how many Ropemakers had lost their jobs since the hanging of Tinkys was stopped? All very well for the Tinkys, but these men had families to feed. Tinky, realising he was no match for Sticky Tam, just told him to away and shite.

    So Louie had left them to it and decided to head home. He hadn't eaten since early afternoon and was feeling a bit peckish, which was bad enough, but the smell from Dora's chip shop was making things worse. He fought off the impulse to go and get something and went upstairs to his house, got into his pyjamas, had a pee, went to bed, had a fag, put the light off, farted, pulled the covers up to smell it, and finally, got himself into a comfy position. As he drifted off to sleep, he could still smell the aroma of frying from Dora's coming in the window. With this smell still in his nose, Louie finally conked out.

Far into the night, Louie was wakened suddenly by someone prodding him. When he came to, he looked round and saw that he was in a small, bare walled windowless room, very like a prison cell. There were three men standing looking at him, one in a suit and two in dark blue uniforms with peaked hats. The man in the suit was reading from a piece of paper something about his appeal for a reprieve had failed and he was to hang by the neck until he was dead the next morning at eight o clock. Louie looked at the three men. He wanted to ask what crime he was to be hanged for? What had he done? To who? When was the trial? How long he had been here? But he found he just couldn't get the words out. The man in the suit then said that as this was the night before his execution, what did he want for his last meal? Louie just sat there stunned into silence, and the man asked again what he wanted: Steak? Roast beef? A bit of salmon? Something exotic, what? At the mention of food, Louie's stomach gave a growl and the saliva of hunger filled his mouth. Louie had had stomach trouble for many years and been told by various doctors that he should stop drinking and eating fried food, particularly chip shop food; something he had a serious liking for. He had decided he would give up one or the other, not both, life just wouldn't be worth living otherwise, so he gave up fried food. Now he was to die tomorrow morning, what did it matter. He ordered fish and chips, a single black pudding and a single pie, all with extra salt and vinegar, four pickled onions, a carton of peas, two buttered rolls and a bottle of Vimto.

The governor sent a warder out to the nearest chip shop to get Louie his order, arriving back an hour or so later. Louie by this time was watering at the mouth at the prospect of tucking into his favourite, and last, meal. He could smell the hot vinegar from the wrapper before the warder even came into the corridor where Louie's cell was located. His mouth was overrunning with saliva by the time the warder came in and laid the parcel of food in front of him. Pushing away the plate the warder had brought for him, Louie spread the wrapper wide open and arranged the contents to his liking with the chips in front, the fish, pudding and onions to either side but within easy reach. He put some chips on one of the rolls, a bit of the fish on the other, then took a long drink of the juice in the peas, savouring with a relish that made him give off a humming sound, he then poured the peas over the remaining chips. Louie picked up the fork and knife that had been laid out for him and started to eat the meal. He made up big forkfuls of fish, chips and peas, then black pudding and chips followed by a bite on one of the rolls, all washed down with the sweet scented taste of the Vimto.

About the time Louie was halfway through this last meal, he suddenly heard the sound of the siren at Halley's mill. Next thing he knew, he was lying in bed looking at the ceiling. When he eventually came to himself, he realised that it had just been another of these strange dreams he had been having lately. When he eventually got up,

Louie went through his usual morning rigmarole ending up with him sitting at the table, fag in hand, tea at the ready and listening to the usual gloom and doom on the wireless. At round about ten past eight, the announcer said that the talked about hanging had taken place. He remembered the dream, and sat thinking about his being in the death cell waiting to be hanged. He sat and thought about this dream for a while, going over in his mind about why he was there? what had he done? was it serious? must have been if they were going to hang him, murder? Was it someone he knew? Then he remembered the meal he was having in the dream, he remembered the nose twitching, mouth watering smell of the hot salt and vinegar combined with the smell of the fish and the chips, the taste of the peas and the first fried fish and black pudding he hadn't eaten in a long, long time. Then, head on hand and fag in hand, Louie suddenly said aloud: ***pity that was just a dream, I was enjoying that, be worth getting hung for***.

XXXIX

At age twelve, I left primary school and was sent to a secondary school. This school, same as the primary, was outside the Rokie. But one story of my time at this school is just too good not to include here.

To describe the particular school that I was going to as a penitentiary is no exaggeration. For one thing, it looked for all the world just like a penitentiary: square cut walls with no ornate or curved lines gave it a negative, institutionalised look. Three storeys high, surrounded by high iron railings and painted a drab beige. The school sat up on a hill where primary pupils for miles around couldn't miss seeing it, it was like a bigger version of Norman Bates house in Psycho.

It was obvious that the local council had used the same architect that had designed Alcatraz. The building was six sided, with the gym halls running through the middle leaving an open space on either side for the exercise yards, sorry, playgrounds, one for girls and one for boys. The only access to either playground was through a 12 foot high archway which was closed off with a huge gate once we were all in.

The school itself was full of all the riff raff of the day: thugs, psychopaths, sadists, and believe me, the pupils weren't much better. Films, comics or books that involved Nazis always drew comparisons with teachers. We knew for a fact that the deputy head was the former commandant of Buchenwald.

Every day started the same, teachers would come out blowing whistles and shouting at us to get in line, all they needed was guns and a few Dobermanns. Once in line, it was orders to stand to attention, then turn right, mark time, then with your right hand on the shoulder of the boy in front, quick march into the school. Any attempt at whistling Colonel Bogey, and there were a few, was met with swift and brutal retaliation, even if it meant belting every boy in the school.

This use of the belt was permitted in schools at this time, and was endemic in this particular school. The slightest thing and the belt was out, talking, not talking, smoking, not having gym shoes, having gym shoes that were the wrong colour, burping, coughing the wrong way, farting meant particularly severe punishment, the list was endless. One thing though, the teachers were not prejudiced, they battered everybody. I once counted up and reckoned we got more physical punishment in three years than prisoners in even the toughest prisons.

As for the education side, well, I went in being able to read, write and do basic arithmetic. Three years later, I left with the same abilities, plus I could put on a bookies line, make a roll up and was pretty good at necking with girls. Not much for three of my most formative years. It was supposed to be a technical based education with an emphasis on the wood and metal trades. Four periods a week each of woodwork, metalwork and technical drawing, in all, 12 X 45 minute periods every week. That mean nearly 1000 hours in the three years I was there. In that time I made a toothbrush rack and a small bookcase with wood, a toothbrush rack and a garden hoe with metal. Bad enough, but I lived in a tenement with no garden, and like most folk at the time, had a mouthful of rotten teeth, so not much use for a toothbrush, let alone a choice of racks to keep it in. As for technical drawing, what's that? I never saw the teacher the entire time I was there, not even sure who it was supposed to be. I just knew that his nickname was JoJo for some reason or other. Probably by boys from past years. One Saturday, me and my big cousin went to the football. Our local team was playing Invercockaleekie neepwallipers or something in the cup. As we went down the terraces looking for a space, he said hello to some bloke in the passing. He then asked if I knew who that was, I said no, and he informed me it was JoJo, the technical drawing teacher. So that's what he looked like!

As for the pupils, there were some real tough cases at the school. Smoking, drinking, stealing, fighting, extortion, gambling, plunking and vandalism were assumed to be on the curriculum, and despite the penalties, were an everyday event. Fights in particular were common, usually about the pettiest things, and occasionally we would have fights with boys from other schools, though we didn't have a clue why. This kind of behaviour was not just confined to the school however, and every so often a boy would disappear only for us to find out later that he had been put in approved school or borstal.

Dress was based on the financial status of parents. As most were skint, only the better off usually wore some semblance of a uniform, but in general, as most had only had one set of clothes, what you wore to school was what you would wear every other day or night of the week, or even to special occasions, trousers, shirt, jacket and shoes of various material, colours, and age. So, between the indifference and brutality of teachers at the school, and the indifference and brutality of the pupils towards each other, it wasn't a place for the faint hearted or those who were there to learn.

So, there it was, and into this all us new 12 year olds were thrown. Of course, the older boys had filled us with grisly tales of torture and pain, which just heightened our sense of foreboding. I knew some of the others that were starting that day, some had been at my primary and so it was safety in numbers as boys tended to huddle in groups of former classmates. This was also the first time I ever set eyes on Jim.

How do you go about describing somebody like Jim? He was standing just slightly away from a group of boys that I took to be his primary classmates. He looked for all the world like an overgrown 5 year old on his first day at primary, not secondary, and especially not this secondary. His hair was tousled with some signs that he had at least tried to comb it, and round his mouth was evidence to the fact that he had had toast and jam for his breakfast. His shirt, trousers and jacket were very clean, in fact spotless, apart from some breakfast jam on his shirt, but they had never been anywhere near an iron. Half the buttons on his shirt were undone, his tie was all to one side, his trousers zip was down with a bit of shirt sticking out, his jacket collar was turned inside, one shoelace was undone and his shirt tail was hanging out. Jim was clean alright, too clean, compared to the rest of us. Mind you, there were some at the school who still had bits of afterbirth stuck to them, so it wouldn't take much to look clean among this lot. But Jim was clean, and I always remember that about him, he looked like he'd been dressed by a blind man with hooks for hands, but him and his clothes were always well scrubbed.

As it turned out, Jim and me were to be in the same class. I slowly got to know a little about him as the first year of secondary got under way. Not only did Jim look like a 5 year old, he also seemed to have the mental and emotional age of a 5 year old. He always had a Beano or a Dandy in his pocket, always had a continuous supply of sweeties and crisps and the like, and once brought a cowboy gun to school with him. He only talked if somebody talked to him first, and only if it was about how the Lone Ranger or Lenny the Lion were getting on these days.

At the PT classes, Jim was totally dependent on the goodwill of his classmates. We would tie his gym shoe laces for him, and try to get his long gym shorts adjusted so that he didn't have one leg of his underpants hanging below the hems. After the class it was the same. We'd do up his shirt buttons and his tie, tuck in his clothes and pull up his zip, do his shoelaces for him and generally tidy him up.

Bullying was never an issue for Jim, we didn't do it, and if anybody else tried, we'd have battered them to a pulp. When we moved up the years, younger boys who tried it on with Jim in the playground were given one warning, it was usually enough. So, in among this scene from the exercise yard at Alcatraz, Jim would wander about virtually unnoticed, shuffling along on his untied shoes, with a comic sticking out of his jacket pocket, eating a packet of crisps or a bar of chocolate, most of which was around his mouth.

Jim had a big problem though, one not made any easier by the fact that he was at a school where belting was compulsory. Jim just couldn't handle getting the belt. It was not that he ever did much to get belted for, he didn't, but that was no escape. There was still the issue of entire classes or even the whole school being belted for one reason or other. Given this schools record, despite the fact that Jim never ever did anything, he got belted quite a few times during his time at the school. It was heartbreaking to see, Jim would be on the verge of tears before he even held his hand out. As soon as he did, his chin would quiver and his head and knees would start shaking, then when the belt landed, the tears would start. Some teachers would leave it at one, even though others got more, but the sadists would always go on to two or three, and once, four. Jim would be in tears and sob for hours afterwards, and on more than one occasion, all the way home on the bus. This would break the hearts of even us roughnecks, and we knew from experience nothing would console him. We all swore revenge on the teacher responsible, but any plots, like the one to put Syrup of Figs in the staffroom tea urn, usually fizzled out. Jim, same as the rest of us, would just have to suffer it for the next three years.

And for the next three years, that's just what happened. Right through first and second year, any excuse to give the belt was taken. Raids on the toilets to catch smokers meant anybody in the toilet got belted, whether they were smoking or not, something that Jim got caught up in now and again. The result of this was that anybody actually needing the toilet done it anywhere but the toilet, which they also got hammered for. One boy got four strokes for failing an arithmetic test, then got it again when he passed the retake of the same test. Another boy got the same for not eating cooked turnip at the school dinners, while the boy he gave it to got the same for eating it. These logic baffling incidents went hand in hand with the usual beltings for the usual suspects for the usual things, you name it, teachers would find a reason to dish out punishment for it.

One day, every boy in the school got belted because it was raining. When it rained, the drill was we had to go under the shelters, not of our own accord however, we had to stand out in the rain and wait to be told, then go to the shelters in an orderly manner. This particular day, a thunderstorm started just as we were going into the school before nine. It was so heavy we all went right into the shelters, to do otherwise meant getting absolutely soaked, even if you had waterproofs on, it was so heavy. When the teachers came out to get us into lines we were all under the shelters. They came at us with whistles shrieking, arms waving and shouting at us to get out into the playground and line up and wait for the order to go to the shelters. We trooped out to the soaking playground, got into lines, stood to attention when ordered, then went back to the shelters when told to. If we thought this was all bizarre, what happened next was like being in an episode of the Outer Limits. The teachers on playground duty that day came round the classes and belted ever boy in turn. As this took a bit of time, some of the classes moved on to their next class before they had finished. The result of this was that the teachers in question belted the same classes twice. It was no use trying to tell them, they just said they had to make sure, better to do it twice that let anybody escape. Poor Jim, just like the rest of us, had to take it. The most harmless, least offensive person you could ever meet went home sobbing at least once a week.

By the time we got halfway through third year, a few of us were looking forward to leaving and starting work. Quite a few had apprenticeships lined up through fathers and uncles in their trade, and some had signed up for the army or the navy, who took 15 year olds at the time. Some already had jobs of sorts at nights and weekends, and so had become a bit independent, buying their own clothes and having money for packets of 20 fags rather than just the five packet or singles that we had been used to. We were also getting a bit sick of all this teacher aggression. It was not so much the belting or the pain, as much as the belittlement and humiliation involved. After one particular class, when seven of us were hammered because somebody in the general area had farted and the rest of us laughed, plots were hatched.

The first was against an elderly teacher, who allegedly taught Maths. We pushed and pushed till he decided to belt the whole class. After getting the belt, the plot was to go to the back of the queue and get it again, and if necessary again, while at the same time making sure Jim didn't get it. 10 minutes later, the teacher was struggling to lift the belt, was red in the face and struggling for breath. He told us all to sit down, only for us to kick up a fuss that it wasn't fair that some boys had got belted and some hadn't. He then left the room and we roared with laughter which was short lived. He returned with the deputy head, he of Buchenwald fame, who ordered us out into the corridor. We were then let back in one at a time where we were given two each, so no escaping. With careful planning, we tried to keep Jim in the class and avoid having him reduced to jelly, but to no avail, Jim spent the next couple of hours sobbing.

Next, we decided to steal as many of the teachers belts as we got a chance to. Not that it made any difference, they just borrowed one till the new ones arrived or kept records of what you were due and gave it when they were rearmed. All through the year this war of attrition went on, with neither side looking like backing down. The more we gave, the more they dished out. In one class, we had taken to having a sweepstakes on who get the most in one class, which was soon tumbled to and we started getting sent down to the deputy head instead. All through this, we did our best to protect Jim from the worst excesses of this conflict. He had to take his licks when it was unavoidable, but all in all, he got off with the worst of it.

Then something absolutely unexpected and amazing happened, something that would initially leave us stunned with disbelief. In fact, so unexpected, that if anybody had told us before that it would happen, we would refuse point blank to believe them. We were in a maths class, supposedly doing Algebra, which as usual, was a complete waste of time, that even the teacher accepted. He had set us some problems, if you wanted to do them, fine, if you didn't, just sit and do what you like, as long as it was quietly, which suited him and us. There was a game of three card brag going on at the far corner, some were playing hangman or reading commando books, and one boy had managed to get his head out of a window unnoticed and was having a fly smoke, and Jim, as usual, was sitting reading the Hotspur. He was also eating a packet of crisps, not something that easy given the racket they make. This was a trick that Jim, along with all the other crisp addicts, had developed to perfection over the years. It was also considered to be a heinous crime, the school equivalent of a hanging offence. It was probably just pure coincidence, but the teacher looked up at exactly the right angle and moment to see Jim stuffing a load of Smokey Bacon into his mouth. Jim was ordered out to the front of the class as the teacher got his belt out of the desk drawer. As usual, Jim was shaking and on the verge of tears as he walked to the front and put the remains of his crisps in the bin as ordered. He held up his hand and the belt came down on it with a thwack, again another thwack as the second stroke landed. To our amazement, Jim's chin was twitching and his head shaking, but no sign of the usual cry of pain or flood of tears. You could see he was as close as he could get to it, but he just turned and walked back to his seat. The look on his face was priceless, a mix of astonishment and pain, but more than that, a look of pride in himself. We, on the other hand, sat in utter astonishment. All the heads slowly turned and followed Jim in his walk back to his seat. Next thing, we were all grinning and whispering about this amazing turn of events, even The teacher looked gobsmacked, but not as much as when he saw what happened next.

Five minutes later, the bell rang for the end of the day. When this happened, we were usually eager enough to get out of the class and the school and start heading home. This time we were champing at the bit, our initial reaction to Jim's belting had turned to excitement, and instead of the usual queuing and waiting at the door to be let out, we just rushed out into the corridor and headed en masse for the outside doors dragging everybody coming out of other classes along with us. The word spread like wildfire about how Jim had got the belt and didn't cry and other boys were joining in the scrum as we headed for the main door. Once outside, Jim was lifted shoulder high and carried along in the mass of boys who had now joined in. The racket of all the cheering and shouting was deafening, and some boys started to tear up jotters and books and throw the scraps of paper into the air. The whole thing had turned into something resembling a hero's welcome out of a Hollywood film, all that was needed was a brass band and some banners and flags. We headed out of the school and crossed the road brushing aside the crossing warden and carrying along anyone who happened to be in the way. Down the road towards the bus stops we headed, people were hanging out of their windows gaping at the spectacle, and looking around we could see the baffled faces of the teachers at the school windows. Hundreds of V signs were given in the direction of the school and a couple of teachers returned them. We didn't give a damn about the consequences, or their belts, why should we. Now that they couldn't even make Jim cry.

XL

Camping, one of life's great delights, especially to a Laddie living in the middle of a big city. Sitting round the fire, sleeping out, just like in the Cowboy films. Or so we thought.

So, there we were one Friday afternoon at the start of the autumn fast. There was myself, wee Dode, Ronnie, Davy, Luca, Gorgi and a boy from Blackscroft called Croftie. We were on about the fourth set of the game of pigeon tennis we had been playing, and it was us 4 pigeons 0. The sound of someone shouting from along the Lane made us look up, and we saw that it was the voice of Sticky Tam who was walking towards us in the company of Tinky McLaren. Sticky came right up to us, and then asked if we would like to go camping. Camping? Of course we would, we told him. Okay, said Tam, and told us to go home and ask our folks if we could go till Monday. That wouldn't be a problem, our folks would all be glad to have of us out of the house for a couple of days. He also told us to meet him at his yard and to bring a blanket and two bob each.

Half an hour later, we're all at Sticky's yard sitting on the back of Eck McLaren's coal lorry waiting for the off. About ten minutes later, Sticky Tam, Tinky McLaren and Frankie McPhee came out of the house carrying essentials for any camping trip, two crates of screwtops. Daft Johnny then came out of the house carrying a crate of Pineappleade, he threw the crate up on the back then went back into the house. He then came back with a big cardboard box and threw that too up on to the back of the lorry. A look in the box revealed a huge load of Tyree's pies and mixed tea bread. Sticky Tam obviously knew his stuff about this camping malarkey. Frankie and Tam then brought out from the big shed what we took to be a tent. There was a huge pole about eight feet long, and a huge pile of canvas that took the two of them to carry. They threw the lot on the back of the lorry, and told us to mind they didn't fall off. Daft Johnny then put Tinky's dog, sputnik, up on the back beside us, then climbed up himself. Tam, Tinky, and Frankie then got in the cab, and with Tam driving, we backed out of the yard and set off.

Tam headed the lorry into town, then took the road that led north out of the city and out to wherever we were going. The first thing we did after setting off, was to stand facing the way we were going with our arms lying on the top of the cab, shouting and waving at everybody and anybody, even dogs. A Boabee on points duty got the full version of the street song ***wha'd like to be a***

Boabee, dressed in Boabees claes, and a big fat boy nearly fell of his message bike as we showered him with gochils as the lorry flew past him. We looked back and saw him shaking his fist and shouting at us, but we were oblivious. Soon, we were out in the sticks, and couldn't pass a cow or a sheep without mooing and baaing at them. Same in the small towns and villages we passed through, everybody got a mouthful. Then we realised that there were a couple of half full sacks of coal dross on the lorry. That was it, cows, sheep, hens, scarecrows, bins, windows, doors, and folk on bikes were bombarded with small bits of the dross. The best however, was when a couple of toffs in tweed suits and funny hats overtook us in an open top car. The shower of coal and gochils that flew at them was like the volley of arrows the Persians fired at the 300 Spartans at the battle of wherever it was. We knew, cos we'd seen it at the show. After they passed, they slowed down, signalling to Tam to stop, obviously to remonstrate about our assault on them. But Tam just waited till they stopped and drove round them and away. Which meant they just got another dose of coal and gochils. They then started to come after us, but obviously thought better of it after a still warm Tyree's pie splattered across the car windscreen, courtesy of Croftie. The car swerved a bit and stopped, then faded into the distance and we never saw them again. Further up the road, a load of choochters got the same treatment when Tam overtook the bus they were all sitting on. This lasted a good way up the road till we run out of coal, and got a bit fed up with the constant wind blowing in our hair and faces, so we sat back down for the rest of the journey.

An hour later, after turning off the main road and driving down a narrow road for a few miles, Tam turned the lorry into a narrow dirt track. The lorry bounced along the track for a bit, then arrived at what was obviously a farmyard. There was an old cottage, a couple of ramshackle wooden buildings and an old rusty tractor with all four tyres flat, and in one corner of the yard, there was a pile of rust eaten farm machinery with weeds growing up around and through them. As Tam steered the lorry into the yard, hens, dogs and a couple of very dirty looking pigs went running in all directions trying to keep out of its way. There was also a burn running along the side of the yard with a wooden bridge that had been made out of what looked like old railway sleepers.

Goin up the country, do you wanna go

When the lorry finally stopped, an old man appeared at the cottage door and surveyed us. He looked ancient and was dressed in what we thought was a very funny way. His bonnet sat at an angle on his head, and the peak had been pulled round to just above his right eye. He was wearing big tackety boots, baggy breeks with bits of string round his legs just below his knees, and an open waistcoat with his thumbs stuck in the pockets. Once everybody got down from the lorry, the old boy, who turned out to be the farmer, walked towards us very slowly with the aid of a walking stick. It was obvious Tam and him knew each other as they called each other by first names, the old boys being Wull. It was obvious that he also knew Tinky, Frankie and Daft Johnny. Tam then introduced us simply as the laddies. Pointing with his stick, and talking out of the side of his mouth in a broad choochter accent, he told us to put up the tent on a bit of flat, grassy ground just at the other side of the bridge.

About an hour or so later, after a lot of effort, sweating, cursing and swearing, the tent was finally set up and ready for occupation. It was obvious the farmer didn't like the thought of us trailing in and out of the cottage, so we had to arrange for our own cooking, washing and the like ourselves. Tinky McLairen then told a couple of us to bring some stones up from the burn for a fire ring, and the rest of us to go and look for wood for the fire. According to the farmer, the water in the burn was okay to drink as long as we didn't take the water from down past the cottage. We were a bit puzzled by this, but soon found out the reason when we were introduced to the toilet facilities. Basically, said Wull, we could pee anywhere, but going for a shite was a different matter, as we were to find out. He took us back to the cottage and round the side, where we were confronted by the sight of what to us was just a small shed. It was only a couple of feet square, tall enough to just stand up in and had a big round hole in the door about head height. On opening the door, we could see that the toilet consisted of a wooden board with a big hole in it sitting over an old bucket. Stuck on a nail in the back of the door was some bits of newspaper cut into small squares. Nothing new here, this was what we had at home. As it turns out, before the farm had a proper toilet and septic tank installed, this was what the farm toilet consisted of. Wull then told us that before using it, to make sure there was water in the bucket, then just chuck the contents in the burn. He obviously expected us to be taken aback by all this, but what we had at home wasn't much better. Besides, we had all seen toilets like this in the cowboy films, and were looking forward to using it. So, there we were, all set for a cowboy style camping weekend.

    The Friday night was all we expected a camping trip to be. We were shown around the farm and told all about what was what. Apart from a few hens, there didn't seem to be much in the way of animals. The outbuildings were a bit shabby, and what machinery there was, was quite rusted and looked like it hadn't been used in years. After the tour, we were allowed to have a game of cowsirs in an old barn. It was perfect, the barn was made of timber, and had an upper floor with a door that led directly outside with an old pulley above it. This was just like in some of the cowboy films we had seen. Later on, we sat round a fire and ate pies and teabread washed down with Pineappleade. That night, we all slept in the big tent dreaming of cowboys on the trail.

Next day, we were awoken early on by Tam who told us to get up, do our whatever we did in the mornings stuff and wait in front of the tent. Quarter of an hour later, Wull brought out a huge pot of tea along with a tray with a mountain of toast, boiled eggs and jam. We all got tore in and in no time had demolished the lot. Tam then told us to follow him, which we did and next thing we were in a field of what I took to be cut down long grass. The grass, which turned out to be hay, was lying in long rows the length of the field. We were each told to stand at the end of a row of hay. Then, Tam said, we were to gather up the hay as we walked along bent over. We did as we were told and started to gather up the hay. When we got a good size bundle, Tam said, we were to leave it and start another bundle. When we started the next bundle, I looked back and Tam, Frankie, Johnny, Tinky and Wull were tying up the bundles.

The long and short of this was that Tam had been at the farm a few days before looking for wood for kindling. He had got talking to the farmer, and on finding out that his machinery was no longer any use, he had done a deal with him to get his harvest in. Of course, we had no idea of this when we were offered a weekends **"camping"**. It took us all day Saturday and most of Sunday to get the hay in, and by the time we got home on Monday afternoon, we were totally knackered. When I told my Granddad about this, he had a good chuckle to himself and asked if Tam had gave us anything. I told him he had went into the nearby village and brought us back a poke of chips, a bottle of lemonade and a bar of chocolate each. At least we had got something said Granddad. ***Got something?*** I shouted ***ee chairged wiz twa bob each fir thim.***

XLI

Sticky Tam was a great one for a laugh. He was the kind of bloke that could see virtually the funny side of anything. And he especially loved a practical joke. One he played in particular one time, near landed him in the jail.

Tam's jokes usually consisted of innocent enough stuff. Like when a self-service shop opened in Albert Street, Tam saw this as an opportunity for some fun. Tam would go into the store and pick up some items that he had no intention of buying. He would then hang about near the checkouts looking like he was browsing. Then he would wait for a victim. When the victim was waiting to get their stuff on to the checkout, Tam would slip something, usually something embarrassing, into their basket. When the victim went into the checkout, all of a sudden their non purchase would be put through, or they would find it and try to explain that it wasn't theirs really. These items were usually the likes of condoms in some ancient old boys basket, or a half bottle of cheap whisky in some stern faced old wifeys. thIs could be a lot of fun, according to Tam, especially when the checkouts were busy.

Another of Tam's tricks was to put up posters on shop windows. These would be along the lines of **CLOSING DOWN SALE! EVERYTHING HALF PRICE!** To do this, Tam would get one of us bairns to go in and buy something to distract the shopkeepers attention. One time, he went up very early in the morning and put a sign up on a shop window with a list of price cuts like. **ALL FAGS HALF PRICE! WHISKY 5/- A BOTTLE!** This one especially caused a stir. When the owner turned up to open at nine o clock, there was a queue stretching halfway down Princes Street. On another occasion, a butcher who was genuinely closing down and had put up a poster advertising half price meat, couldn't understand why nobody wanted it.

Tam was also a great one for getting back at those he thought were just too full of self importance. In particular, Tam had it in for those who wrote antagonistic letters to the newspapers. One typical letter writer who complained about the usual **YOUTH OF TODAY,** couldn't understand why he was suddenly being bombarded with phone calls offering to buy a monkey he didn't have. Tam had put an ad in the same paper offering the monkey with the writers phone number. Another letter writer came home to find a ton of coal in his driveway, and a demand for payment from one of the city's biggest suppliers. The best however, was when a particularly nasty letter, demanding the reintroduction of the birch, resulted in the writer being sent umpteen books and utensils usually used by those into S&M and bondage. Tam had got the info on where these items were advertised from the owner of the nood book shop in Blackscroft. Among the stuff sent were leather items of clothing, belts, chains, whips, canes, and books such as Women in Chains. Best of all was a full size set of stocks sent from a maker in England. The main problem for the letter writer, was first how to explain this to his wife, and then how to get rid of the stuff. Not that simple! If he put it in the bin, then the scaffies would find it. Also, payments for the stuff on approval would start coming in. If he didn't send it back, they might take him to court.

To us laddies, Tam's **Piece de Resistance** was when he changed the letters around on a shop sign in Princes Street. A Chemist shop opened up on one of the more run down parts of Princes Street. The owner, knowing that he probably wouldn't be there that long, bought a temporary sign. This sign consisted of letters two foot high simply saying **CHEMIST**. The letters were held on to the sign board by screws. Tam went up during the night, and armed with a ladder and a screwdriver, he then changed the word **CHEMIST** to **MC SHITE.** Tam however, eventually played a joke that caused him a lot of trouble, but certainly enhanced his reputation in the Rokie.

The joke in question, didn't actually start out as a joke, but an act of revenge. One time, Tam found that his supply of sticks was dwindling, without him having sold any. He had been laid up with the flu for about a week, but the pile of sticks was diminishing. He noticed that in particular, a big pile of logs was going down steadily. Tam had went out to the country after a storm one time, offering to clear blown over trees for farmers. He had got a lorry load of these logs, and intended to keep them for special customers and his own use. Tam suspected that someone close by was sneaking in to the yard and helping themselves to the logs. So, he went to a shop and bought 2 penny bangers. He then broke them open and got the explosive powder out of them. Then, Tam got a good size log and bored a one inch hole in it with a bit and brace. The powder was poured into the hole, then Tam cut an inch or so off the floor brush handle and sealed the hole. He hammered the bit of handle into the hole, then paired it down with a knife. Once ready, Tam put the log back on top of the pile.

    It took a few days, but eventually it happened. We were out playing in the Hutty, when there was a dull, but very audible bang, more like a thud really. We realised it was coming from along Blackscroft, near to Mackies shop. All of us took off, lowped over the billboards and headed towards the source of the thud. Looking along the street, we could see what we took to be black reek coming from a window above Mackies. When we got there we found it wasn't reek, but soot, and it was coming out of a broken window. Suddenly, a figure came staggering out of the close next to the shop, a black figure cover in soot who was coughing and heching. Suddenly, Sticky Tam, Tnky McLairen and Daft

Johnny appeared. Tam walked right up to the blackened, coughing figure and belted him right in the face.

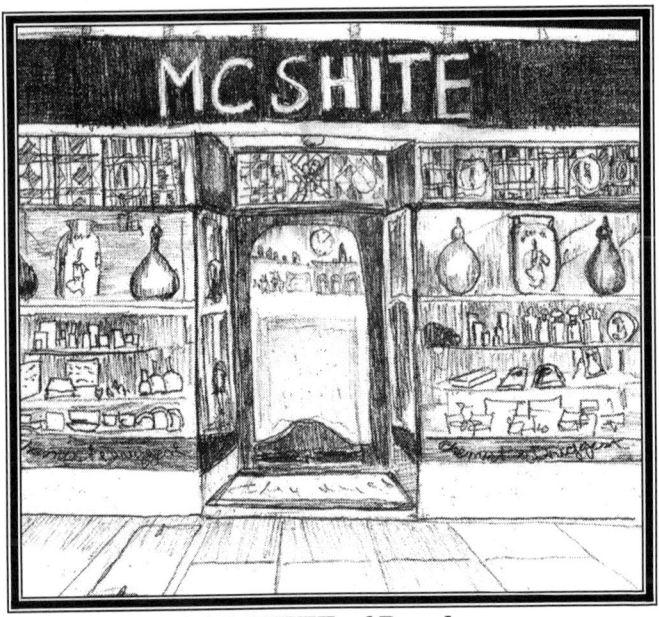

MC SHITE of Dundee

The story of what happened eventually surfaced via Slaberee Alec. The log thief was a boy called Dan Boyle, a well known dosser, drunk, wife beater and one of the most loathed people in the area. He had been evicted from his previous house and had managed to get a house on Blackscroft. He had found a way into Tam's yard through a Close that backed on to the yard from the other side of Blackscroft. When the explosive log had went off, it had blown the grate right out of the fireplace and across the living room. The blast had not only blown out the window, but had caused all the soot in the lum to loosen and come crashing down into the living room. Although no charges were ever brought against either Tam, or Dan Boyle, Tam did get a letter telling him that if they had been brought, he most likely would have got a few months in the jail. Tam was delighted however, he had caught the log thief, and the Rokie had got rid of Dan Boyle.

XLII

Round about the time my auntie Belle knitted me a pair of swimming trunks, Daft Tam found that he was being haunted.

Like most laddies round the area, I learned to swim down at the docks. There was great fun to be had at the docks in the summer, swimming, making rafts and diving, so if you wanted to join in, you had to learn. Also like most laddies, you went swimming in the nude, or in an old pair of breeks. However, when the teacher at school told us that not only were we going to be taken to the baths every Thursday, she also told us we would need trunks and a towel. I told my Gran about needing trunks and she said she would see to it. A couple of days later, she hands me a pair of trunks ok, but they had been knitted by my auntie Belle. For a change, unlike some stuff she knitted, the trunks were all one colour. Fine! I thought, but what do I know.

A good view of my bare arse

That Thursday, we headed from the school to the baths. I put on my new trunks, run out the cubicle and dived in. I started to swim and realised I wasn't going anywhere. Normally, one dive would have taken me clear to the other side of the pool. But here I am not even halfway across. I looked back, and the arse of the trunks was still at the point where I dived in. Worse was to come though. When I climbed up the steps to get out of the pool, though I was on the top step, the arse of the trunks were still on the bottom of the pool. It took about four big pulls before I got them out of the water and up on the poolside. I looked down, and was sure the level of the water had went down. I then started to walk along the side of the pool with the trunks dragging about ten feet behind me, not realising that the entire place was getting a good view of my bare backside. One of the attendants came over to me, and handing me a pair of real trunks, told me to go into a cubicle and change. My Grandad near died laughing that night when I told him what had happened. He asked me where they were, and I said I had left them in the cubicle. He said I should have kept them for the rest when they had to go. Bastard! I never thought of that.

That same night, I was heading up to Dora's when I saw Daft Tam standing in a Close on Blackscroft. I told him about the carry on that day with the trunks, and he told me the same thing happened to him one time with a jersey when he fell in the dock. Next thing I know, Tam suddenly looks across the road and shouts, ***eh see yi, yi ald bastard***! I looked across the road in the same direction as Tam, but the street is empty, and there's nobody at any of the Closes or windows. Tam then went running across the road and up the Close next to the nood book shop. I could hear him shouting at somebody, and went across for a look. Before I got there, Tam had come back out the Close, run down Blackscroft, then turned up Middle Street. I decided I better go and get the message I had been sent for.

When I got back to the house, I told Gran and Granddad about the episode with Tam. Granddad said that he too had noticed that Tam had been acting funny the last while, and no doubt he'd find out all about it next time he was in the pub.

A couple of nights later, the story about Tam's behaviour was revealed. According to the reports that Harry Bradley had gathered, along with his blethers with Tam in the pub, it seemed that Tam was convinced he was being haunted by a Ghost. The Ghost in question being the Ghost of the boy whose grave Tam had fell into that night he was pished. Tam told Harry that the Ghost was a man dressed in funny clothes. He was wearing a long jacket, breeks that came down to his knees with socks that came up to them, and his shoes had a big buckle. His hair was down to his collar, which was combed back on the top of his head. He said that he was dressed like somebody in that film with Gregory Peck, the one where he was a ship's captain, but without the hat. Tam obviously meant Captain Horatio Hornblower, which meant the Ghost was dressed in clothes from the late 18th or early 19th century. Harry had said that this all seemed to fit, the Boneyard on Ferry Road was very old, and no doubt there were graves dating from that time. Tam had then went on to say that the Ghost was always there, out in the street, at his work, in his house, even in the pub. According to Harry, as he was speaking to him, Tam said that the Ghost was sitting on a seat next to the fireplace, staring at him. Harry said he couldn't see anyone. If he saw the Ghost standing at a Close, Tam said he would go over and the Ghost would go up the Close. When he followed it, the Ghost would be at the far side of the backies, when he went there, the Ghost would be back at the Close. It was the same everywhere he went, the Ghost always stayed a few yards ahead of him. One time he had followed the Ghost up a Close and when he got round the back, the Ghost was up at the back of Sticky Tam's yard. He had tried running round to Tam's yard, but when he got there it was back at the Close again. Worst though, said Tam, was when he was in the house at night in his bed. The Ghost would just stand in the corner of the room looking at him. Every time he looked up, the Ghost was there. It never spoke or made any noise, it would just stand there staring at him. Tam had taken to shouting at the Ghost, telling it he could see it, and telling it in no uncertain terms to bugger off.

Whut di yi wahnt, yi ald cunt

For the next few months, Tam could be heard at all times of the day and night shouting the likes off, *awa ti fuck n lave is* **alane** or *whut di yi wahnt, yi ald cunt.* It finally got to the point however, where Tam's neighbours couldn't take any more of the nightly bawling, shouting and cursing. So, one day, same as with daft Margaret, Tam was taken away in the van.

A couple of days later, Granddad was talking to Father Mahon in the allotment. Father Mahon said that things like that did happen to folk who drank as much as Tam, it was called alcohol psychosis, and a spell off the booze could only be good for him. Grandad asked Father Mahon if he could just rule out the Ghost and falling in the grave stuff, to which Father Mahon said yes. Granddad then said *thank goad fir that, eh did the same thing in the same graveyaird fufty year ago.*

XLIII

Cluny had a wee dog that he used to walk every night at the docks. One night, the dog turned up in the Rokie on its own, trailing its lead behind itself. Nobody really took much notice, and just thought it had run away from Cluny, and who could blame it. However, it was still wandering around the next day, still with the lead trailing. Old man Tyree saw it sitting at his door, realising that it was probably hungry and attracted by the smell of his shop. So, he got hold of it and waited on Slaberee Alec coming in for his usual mooch. After his morning repast at the shop, Alec took the dog and walked along to Cluny's house. There was no answer to his knocking, so he took the dog to the police box and call for the dog wardens to pick it up.

After a few days, there was still no sign of Cluny, and the dog was still in the pound. A search was made of the docks and the coast guard alerted to the probability of a body being washed up somewhere. It was about a week later that a body was eventually found washed up on a beach in Fife. It turned out to be Cluny. It was assumed he had fallen in the water somewhere, probably on the quayside, and his body washed away with the tide. The tide tables were checked and they seemed to verify an ebb tide that night. It was also a few days later that folk noticed that Tibor, Luca and Gorgi hadn't been seen around.

A couple of weeks after Cluny's demise, the owner of the second hand furniture shop on Blackscroft got a letter. It turned out to be from Tibor. According to the owner, there was a key, and a note telling him to help himself to the contents of the house, then hand in the key to the landlord. The postmark on the letter said it had been posted in Hungary.

Of course this started all the amateur Sherlock Holmes putting two and two together. Before they left, according to the sleuths, Tibor and Luca had went down the docks, waited for Cluny, then either threw him off the quayside into the fast flowing water, or drowned him in the old slipway and threw him into the river. They had then taken Gorgi and buggered off to Hungary. Most folk, on hearing the various stories, just said good on them and wished them all the best. Sticky Tam summed it up best though. *Will ah be laving here sain enuff, but tull wi do, the Rokie'll be a better place.*

So, there it is.

FAREWELL
TO
ST ROQUES

The Illustrated Dundee Dictionary

Abbreviations used in the text:
Alt   Alternative. May be used in place of the word.
M   Multiple. The word has more than one use.
Pr   Pronounced. How letter or word is sounded

The Colossus of Dundee stood at the harbour entrance. Demolished in 1962.

A

Abdee Everybody.
Aboot About.
Abrode Abroad **Alt: Ibrode.**
Ach Sound of sudden annoyance
Ae One. **eg:** I went to the match **Ae** time".
Aff Off.
Affy Awful **Alt: Saffy**
Afore Before. **Alt: Ifore.**
Ah All. Every.
Ahent Behind
Ahin Everything. **Alt: Athin.**
Aibirdeen Aberdeen.
Aipil Apple.
Airm Arm. As on the body not as in weapon. **Alt: Erm**
Airms Arms. Plural of Arm, not the weapons.
Airy M AeropLane. Cool weather.
Alane Alone. **Alt: ILane.**
Aloe Below. **Alt: Iloa.**
Ana As well. Too.
Andri Familiar name for Andrew.
Ane M: One. Own. **eg:** 'mind your **ane** business".
Ald Old
Aldir M Older. Singular of **Aldirz.**
Aldirz Day old Bakery goods bought for half price.

Amblayins Ambulance.
Aplace All places.
Argee: Argue.
Argeed Argued.
Argee-in Arguing.
Aridee Already.
Arite Alright. **Alt: Aricht.**
Athigithir Altogether.
Athin Everything **Alt: Ahin.**
Atween Between. **Alt: Itween**
Awa Away.

B

Ba Ball.
Backerties Backwards. The action of going Backwards.
Backies Area of ground at back of tenements.
Backy The act of giving someone a lift on a bike. (Punishable by law)
Bah-ir M Batter. Crispy matter round fried fish etc. To hit multiple times.
Bah-ired M Battered. Past tense of **Bah-ir**
Bahl M Bawl: as in to cry out loud. Ball: a dance.
Bahlin Bawling
Bahltic M Baltic: The sea off N. Europe. A flax mill in Dundee up to 1980. Very cold.

Bahl: A dance for Posh rich fowk

Baird Beard
Bairn A child.
Bam Big headed person. Common throughout Scotland, but in Dundee used with words 'pot' and 'stick' to give **Bampot/Bamstick.**
Bampot Big headed, conceited person. See **Bam.**
Barkit Dirty.
Barry Barrow
Bamstick Alt for **Bam/Bampot.**
Bathir Bother.
Bathired Bothered.
Bathirin Bothering.
Bayst Beast.
Bayt **M** To beat someone at a game. Boot.
Bayth Both
Bayts **M.** Beats. Boots. Previously very common in Dundee. People in Dundee did not wear shoes till 1960s, even women and children.

Baz Balls. Plural of Ball.
Beelin Poisoned. But Only when referring to the finger. **eg.** " I have got a Beelin finger".
Beh Buy. By.
Ben Used mainly in the domestic situation. To move from one room to another.
Bez Used to describe act of buying:
Bide Stay. Live.
Bile **M** Boil, as in Boil the kettle. A Boil on the back of the neck. Also the name Boyle.
Bile-in **M** Boiling. The act of to boil. A sweet made of boiled sugar.
Bile-t Boiled same as **Bile**, but with T on end, sometimes with D: **Biled.**
Birl Turn
Birlin **M:** Turning. A form of local dance.
Bisim A brush of any kind.
Biy Bay.
Blackie A Dundee street and school.
Blah **M:** Blow. As in the wind.
Blah-in **M:** Blowing. What a boaster does.
Blaiss Bless.
Blaz **M:** Blows. Only as in the wind, or a boaster.
Blethir Person who talks a lot.

Blethired Past tense of **Blethir**
Blethirin Act of to **Blethir**. **eg:** A Blethirin Erse, a person who talks a lot.
Blihnd Blind. **Pr:** As in wind.
Blihndee Royal National Institution for the Blind.
Blihndz Blinds
Boab Familiar for Robert.
Boabee Policeman.
Boabeez. Plural of **Boabee.**
Boadee Body.
Boadeez Bodies.
Boaly **M** Outside cellar usually under stairs. Partitioned section of public house.

Robert (Boab) Peel, the man who invented the Boabeez.

Boardir Border.

Boarn Born.
Bocht Bought. **Pro:** ch as in Loch.
Booxed Pre-select. **eg.**I **Booxed** a window seat".
Boney **M** Bonfire.
Bool Singular Marble or Bowl. See **Boolz.**
Boolz **M** Marbles, as in the game. Bowls, as in the game.
Borry Borrow.
Borried Borrowed
Borry-in Borrowing
Bowfin Strong, bad smell.
Bowil Bowl, as in soup bowl, **Pr:** same as bowels.
Bra Very good.
Braid Bread.
Braith Breath
Brak Break.
Breenj To approach or attack suddenly.
Breest Mammary gland.
Breests Plural of mammary gland.
Bren Brain.
Brenny Brainy.
Brenz Brains.
Brer Brother. **Alt: Brithir.**
Brinkehtis Bronchitis
Brithir Brother. **Alt: Brer.**
Brithir in lah Brother in law
Brode Broad.

Albert Einstein was Very Brenny

Broo M Hair above eye. Place to sign on if unemployed.
Broon Brown. The colour or name,.
Brooz Plural of **Broo.** Hair above the eyes.
Bucky Place where workman take their breaks.
Buhl M Bull. Bill, as in electric bill.
Buhloo The colour Blue.
Buray Bury.
Burayd Buried.
Bumir Factory siren
Bunce Pool resources. eg: Lets **Bunce** up and buy a carry out
Burd M Bird. Any species of Bird. Girlfriend. Young woman.
Burday Birthday. **Alt: Burthday.**
Burdz Plural of Bird.
Burthday Birthday. **Alt: Burday**.

But M Bit. **eg**. 'The dog **But** me'. A piece of something. **eg.** 'Would you like a **But** of cake?'.
Buty M: Same as in a piece of something. **eg:**. 'Would you like a **Buty** cake?'. A unit of distance. **eg** 'It is a good **Buty** to the nearest pub'.

Casanova had loads of Burdz

C

Ca M Call: **eg** "I will **Ca** you what I like". To turn something round and round, mainly ropes when skipping, see **Fiyreez**.
Cad M Called: **ie**. 'She cad me a **Tink**'. Past tense of turning something round and round. See **Ca**
Ca-in M Calling: **ie**.

"He kept ca-in me Hugh, and my name is Shug". The act of turning something round and round. See **Ca**.
Caird Card.
Cairdz **M:** Cards. A shop that was in Reform St.
Cairn Caring.
Cald Cold. Both the temperature and the illness.
Canni Cant: **eg** I **Canni** do it. Not the German Philosopher. Alt: **Canny.**
Canny **M:** Cant. A gentle person, or doing something in a gentle manner. **Alt: Canni.**
Carpenter Person who paints cars
Cassie Granite or whinstone block used in road making.
Cerrij Carriage.
Cha Chew.
Chad Chewed. Not the country in Africa.
Cha-in Chewing.
Chas Chews.
Cha-ay Food that takes a lot of chewing. Alt: **Chooch.**
Chaip Cheap. Only as in the low price of an item. Not the sound made by a budgie.
Chairj Charge.

Generally only used in terms of money, or after arrest by Boabeez.
Chairjed Charged.
Chairy High diving board at swimming baths. As in old childrens rhyme: Mary had a little lamb, she also had acanary, she took them to the Lochee baths and they bothjumped the **Chairy.**
Chait Cheat. Both the act and the person. **Alt: Swick**
Chaitin Cheating
Chaitit Cheated.
Chanter Singer.
Chanty Toilet bowl.

Sir John Harington Invented the Chanty in 1596

Chap Chop. The act of chopping, not as in a Pork Chop.
Chapped Chopped. Past

tense of Chop.
Chapper Used with "**Uppir**" to create "**Chappir Uppir**" A person who went round knocking on doors early in the mornings to waken people up for work. A small fee was paid for this service.
Chappin M Chopping. The act of to chop. Term used in the game of Dominos when a participant cannot proceed due to a lack of dominos of the appropriate suit.
Cheenj Change.
Chickymelly Childs game involving knocking on doors and running away. Now called Parcel Force.
Chist Chest.
Choochtir A person of rural origin. See **Farfir.**
Chooch Meat that is tough. **Pr:** last ch as in loch. **Alt: Cha-ay**
Choonee Chewing gum.
Chucky A small stone.
Chummy sait Double seat at the cinema used by courting couples. **Alt: Dev-on**
Cla Claw. Scratch.
Cla-in Scratching. Act of To scratch.
Clad Scratched.
Claiz Clothes.

Claz M Claws. Scratches. Claus. As in Santa, the person who comes at Christmas.
Click One of a pair of people who meet for the first time on a romantic basis.
Cloot A piece of cloth used for wiping or drying dishes.
Close Common entry to tenement.
Clubee Club. As in social club. Clubee book.
Clup Clip.
Clupped Clipped
Cluppin Clipping.
Cluppirs Clippers.

Harrods: where posh fowk buy their Claiz

Coad Cod.
Coard Cord.
Coarn M Corn, as in Corn Flakes. Corn, as on foot.
Coarnz Plural of Corns.

250

Coarnir Corner.
Comfay Come from. **eg:** 'Where do you **Comfay**.?'
Conshy Constitution road, a Dundee street.
Coonsul Council.
Coont **M** Count. To add up. Member of European aristocracy.
Coontin Counting. The act of counting.
Coontit Coontit. Past tense of coont.
Coontir Counter. As in where customers are served in shops.
Coort **M** Court. To have a romantic relationship with person of opposite sex. Where villainous persons get their comeuppance.
Coortin Courting. The act of being involved in a romantic relationship.
Coortit Past tense of Court.
Cowp **M** To turn something over. Place where rubbish is dumped.
Cowped Past tense of Cowp.
Cowsir A cowboy film.
Cra Crow. The bird..
Crab Person who is Always complaining.
Crabbit Always complaining.
Cral Crawl
Crallin Crawling

Crallir Crawler. A sycophant.
Creh **M** Call. Cry
Crehd **M** Called. Cried
Creh-in **M** Calling, Crying.
Cubbij Cabbage.
Cubee hole Place for keeping small personal items.
Cundee Street drain.

D

Dab Hit. As in a **Dab** in the face (pus)
Dachtir Daughter.
Dachtir in lah Daughter in law
Daid Dead.
Daif Deaf.
Daith Death
Dall Doll. Childs toy. Not the buttocks, or good looking girl.
Dally Dolly. Childs toy. Notused to describe good looking girl.
Dandir Singular Cinder. Temper.
Day Do. As in to do something.
Day-in Doing
Ded **M**. Died. Dyed.
Dee Die: To pass away. Word of more **Choochtir** origin.
Deed Died.
Deez Dies.

Dee-in Dying.
Deh M Die. **Alt: Dee.**
Dye. To change the colour of something.
Deh-in Dying.
Deh-it Diet.
Dehmind Diamond
Dennir Dinner.
Der Dire
Derry Diary.
Dev Dive
Devd Dived.
Devin Diving
Devir Person who dives.
Dev-on Double seat at the cinema. **Alt: Chummy sait**
Deez Dies.
Dicht Wipe
Didnae Did not. **Alt: Didni**
Didni Alt: Didnae

Samuel Pepys kept a famous Derry

Dile Doyle **eg:** Arthur Conan Dile
Dinnae. Do not. **Alt: Dinni** Do not. **Alt Dinnae.**

Divee M Divide. Dividend payment tomembers of Cooperative society. See **Sosh**.
Diveed Divided. **eg.** 'We won some money at the bingo, so we **Diveed** it.
Divil Devil.
Diytit Description of a very stupid person.
Diz Does.
Dizin Dozen.
Diznae Does not. **Alt: Dizni**
Dizni Does not. **Alt: Diznae**
Doag Dog.
Doagz Dogs
Doazint Also description of a stupid person.
Dob Steal.
Dobee Object, money etc that has been stolen.
Docky Large stone.

The Docky of Destiny.

Dode Familiar for George.
Doll The Buttocks. **Alt: Dowp. Erse.**
Doo M Pigeon. A party, not political.
Dook To plunge the body or part of, into water.
Dookin The act of plunging into water.
Doolee Singular solid nasal mucus.
Doon Down.
Dooned Downed.
Doot Doubt.
Dootitl doubt it.
Dossir A very lazy person. Often used in conjunction with the word **Loabee.**
Dowp The Buttocks. **Alt: Doll. Erse.**
Dowpee Cigarette end.
Dowpeez Plural of **Dowpee.**
Dra Draw.
Dra-in Drawing
Draclaya Dracula.

Draclaya

Drap Drop.
Drappy A unit of measurement.
Drar Drawer.
Drarz Plural of **drar**. Also a pair of Undergarments.
Draz M Draws. As in on the football pools. Sketches.
Dreh Dry
Drehd Dried
Dreh-in Drying
Dreh-ir Drier
Dreebil Rate of flow of a fluid.
Dreeblin Describing the rate of flow of a fluid.
Dreech Damp weather
Dreel Row. Generally used to describe rows of berries and potatoes at the annual harvest.
Dreep Drip. Also used as unit of measurement.
Dreeped Dripped.
Dreepin Dripping. Also the meat by-product used for frying.
Drev Drive.
Drevin Driving.
Drevir Person who Drives.
Drooblee Football played in the normal manner.
Drookit Very wet.
Droon Drown
Dross M: Loose change. Small bits of coal at

253

bottom of bunker.
Dub A Puddle.

Hippos live in Dubs in Africa

Dubit Divot. Dropped off **Pletty** by children on to victim's head. Also used by children as a form of warfare **eg**. A **Dubit** fight.
Dup Dip. Used with the word **Peece-n,** to describe a local delicacy a **Peece-n dup** where bread is dipped in mince or stew.
Dupped Dipped.
Duppin Dipping.
Duppy A member of the Baptist Church. Originates from the practice of immersing or **Duppin** new members into the waters of the river Tay as a form of Baptism. See also **Duppin.**
Dwahrf Dwarf.
Dwahrf Dwarves.

E

Earik Sore ear.
Echt The number, Eight.
Echteen The number Eighteeen.
Echth Eighth
Echty The number Eighty.
Eck Short for Alexander.
Ecks Belonging to Alexander
Ecky Also short for Alexander.
Ee He. Also alternative word for Eye. **Alt: Eh.**
Eedee-it Idiot.
Eel He will.
Eelnoa He will not.
Een Eyes. See also **Ehz.**
Een Eyes. See also **Ehz.**
Eerik Earache
Eesell Himself

Eck the Great King of Macedonia

Eez He is. **eg**. "Eez going to do it". **Alt: Heez.**

Eeznoa He is not.
Eftir After.
Eftirnane Afternoon.
Eftirwirds Afterwards
Eh M Yes. Eye **Alt: Ee.**
Ehdee-ih Idea.
Ehdeel Ideal.
Ehfuhl Eyeful. Also a Tower in Paris.
Ehl I will
Ehm I am.
Ehv I have
Empehr Empire. A cinema in Dundee till 1950s.
Erchy Short for Archibald. Also, a means of deflating a boaster. **eg.** 'Think your
Erchy then, do you?'
Erm Arm. **Alt: Airm.**
Erse Buttocks. **Alt: Doll. Dowp.**
Et Ate.
Exil Axle.
Express Alexander's cupboard. See **Eck & Press.**
Ez Eyes. **Alt: Een.**

F

Fah Fall
Fah-in Falling.
Fail Fool. Only used to describe someone doing something stupid. **ie:** 'he made a right **Fail** of himself'.

Faird Afraid
Fairdee Person who is afraid. See **Gowk.**
Fals False.
Falsirs False teeth. Very common in Dundee.
Falt Fault.
Farfir Forfar. Place where Choochtirs live. See **Choochtir.**

Fairdee Gowk never won fair lady
Don Quixote

Fay From.
Faz Falls. Only used to describe someone falling. Not as in Niagara.
Febir Fibre.
Fecht Fight.
Fechtin Fighting.
Fechtir Fighter. **eg.** A bonny **Fechtir,** like Oor Wullie.
Feechee Covered in germs.
Feechee touch. A

children'sgame similar to tig. **Feechee** touch is also the Disease that killed 75 million people inEurope between 1348 and 1350, and was also known as The Black Death.The cure for the disease was discovered by children in Dundee in the 1950s, who simply blew on the infected part. **Pr**: ch as in loch.

Feechee touch killed millions of people in the 14th century.

Feenish Finish.
Feenished Finished.
Feenishin Finishing
Fell A bit. Used to describe.
eg. " It is **Fell** cold tonight".
Femly Family.
Fer Fire. **Alt: Fiyir.**
Ferm Farm. Place where **Choochters** live and work.
Fessin Fasten.
Fest Fast. As in the rate of speed. Also the Spring and Autumn weekend holidays. Not to do without food.
Festir Faster.
Festist Fastest.
Fev The number five.
Fevir A five pound note. Rare in Dundee till 1960s.
Fingir Finger. **Pr:** Same as in fling
Fir For. **Alt: Fur.**
Fiyir Fire. **Alt: Fer**
Fiyree Member of the Fire Brigade
Fiyreez M Fire Brigade.Game played with skipping ropes where the rope is turned at very high speed. See also **Cah.**
Flair Floor.
Flairz. M Plural of Floor. Trousers worn in 1970s. May be confused with Distress flares, especially if Bright colours with a high waist and 36 inch bottoms with 3 inch turn ups. Common in Dundee at time.
Fle M To Fly, as in an aeropLane. A Fly, the insect. Sly.
Fle-in The act of Flying.
Fle-ir Flier. Term Commonly used on Bingo nights at social clubs.
Flech Small fly or Flea.

Flee M To hurry. A Fly, the insect.
Flee-in To hurry.
Fleg A fright.
Flet Flat. Only as in beinglevel, not used to describe a flatted dwelling house.
Fletist Flattest.
Flettir Flatter.
Flez M Flies, plural of Fly, the insect. Verb of To Fly. **eg.** "He **Flehz** down to London tomorrow.
Flook M Fluke. Flounder, the fish. Success brought about by luck.
Flookee Action carried out successfully by sheer luck.
Floondir Flounder. The fish. **Alt: Flook.**
Foaty Photograph.
Foatyz Photographs.
Focht M Fought. Not physically, an argument.
Follied Followed.
Folly Follow
Folly-in Following.
Foondry Foundry.
Foostee Slightly mouldy.
Footir To do something with no particular outcome in mind. **eg.** " I think I will go and **Footir** about in the garden."

Footired Past tense of **Footir. eg.** He **Footired** about in the garden all day". See **Footir** and **Footerin.**
Footirin The act of doing something with no particular outcome in mind. See **Footir.**
Fowir The number four. **Pr:** As in Hour.
Fowk Folk.
Fred Fried
Freh Fry.
Freh-in Frying
Freend A relative.
Freendz Plural of **Freend. eg.** "I have got **Freendz** in America".
Frery Friary.
Frez Fries.
Fufteen The number Fifteen
.**Fufty** The number Fifty.
Fufth Fifth.
Fuhl Full.
Fuhlih Full of.

Elizabeth Freh was famous for making chocolate

Fulm Film.
Fund Found.
Fur For. **Alt: Fir.**
Furst First.
Fut **M** Foot. On the end of the leg. The unit of measure. In the unit of measure, **Fut** is also used s the plural. Eg. " The table is three **Fut** long". Fit. As in, does the shirt **Fut** you.
Futba The game of Football,but not the actual ball. See **Tub. Ba.**

G

Gadgie Alt: Mink, Minkir, Tink, Tinky.
Gae Go.Not as in homosexual.
Gae-in Going.
Gaid Went.
Gaird Guard.
Gairdn Garden.
Gais Guess
Gaisais A children's game.
Gal Gall.
Gallisis Braces for holding up trousers.
Gamp Umbrella.
Gaze Goes.
Geeh Give. **Pr: G** as in Goat.

The Hanging Gairdns of Babylon

Geez. Give me. **Pr: G** as in Goat.
Geezit Give me it.
Geh Only used to describe Guy Fawkes.
Gehm Game. **Pr: G** as in go.
Gehzin Traditional display carried out by children on Halloween, similar to American trick or treat.
Gehzir Participant I Halloween display.
Gethir Gather
Girn Moan.
Girned Moaned.
Girnin Moaning.
Girraf Get off.
Git Get.
Giy Very. **eg.** "It is **Giy** Warm today". **Pr:** as in tide.
Glaik Vacant looking person
Glaikit Description of vacant looking person.
Gleebee Glebelands. A Dundee school.

Glesgae Glasgow.
Gless Glass.
Glessis Glasses. Spectacles.
Goad God.
Gochil Spit. The action of forcibly ejecting saliva from the mouth. A singular piece of saliva that has been forcibly ejected from the mouth. Not as in for roasting meat.
Gochils Plural of Spit.
Gochled Past tense of to Spit.
Gochlin The act of Spitting
Goon Gown
Gowk A funny or stupid looking person. Often usedin conjunction with **Fairdee,** to describe someone who is unnecessarily scared.
Gowpin Food that tastes bad.
Greenee Space at rear of tenements, but where grass has been allowed to flourish.
Alt: Backies.
Greet Cry, as in with tears, not to shout. See **Creh.**
Greetin **M** To Cry. Moaning. **eg.** " He is a right **Greetin** faced old person".
Alt: Girnin.

Gret Past tense of Cry. **eg**. "He **Gret** for ages after he got the belt".
Grippit Mean. As with money.
Grippy **Alt: Grippit.**
Grou Grow. **Pr:** as in cow..
Grund Ground.
Grup **M** Grip. Get up.
Gureen The colour Green.
Gutters Mud.
Gymnkhana James cant do it.

H

Hack **M** Hawk. As in to sell something in the street or from door to door. Foul play at the game of Football. Used with **Yir Mutton** to describe person who is going to work as a prostitute. The bird of prey. **ie**. Shitehack.
Hacked **M** Hawked. Past tense of Hack.
Hackie Hawkhill. A Dundee street and school.
Hackin The act of to **Hack.** See **Hack**
Hackir Person who carries out the act of **Hackin**.
Hae Have. **Alt: Hiv.**
Hae-in Having

Fanny Hill used to Hack her mutton in 18th century London

Haffies To take a half each.

Hitler & Stalin went Haffies on Poland in 1939

Haid Head.
Haidee Headmaster at schools.
Haidik Sore head.
Haidir M Header. To fall on the head. To assault another with a head butt. The act of striking the ball with the head in the game of football.
Haidired Past tense of **Haidir.**
Haip Heap.
Hait Heat.
Haivir Person who tells tall stories.
Haivired Past tense of telling tall stories.
Haivirin The act of telling tall stories.
Haivirs Tall stories.
Hal M Haul. Hall. A very large room ie. The Caird **Hal.** Never used to describe the passageway at the back of the front door in houses. They do not exist in Dundee houses, Dundee houses have **Loabees.** See also **Loabee.**
Hale Whole.
Halfcroon Pre decimal coin worth 30 old pennies or 1/8 of a pound. 12 ½ pence in decimal currency.
Halikit Acting in a clumsy manner. **eg**. "He is a right **Halikit** person"
Hame Home.
Havee Haversack. Originally meant for carrying gas masks

during WW2. Used by post war schoolchildren as schoolbags, and by workmen to carry **Peeces**.
Hedroa Hydro.
Heez M his. He is. **Alt: Eez.**
Hefin Hyphen.
Heh High. Often used in conjunction with **Burdee** and
Fleh. See **HehBurdeeFleh.**
HehBurdeeFleh Action carried out by four people who each take an arm or leg of a person, swing them back and forward horizontally then let them go. Often used as punishment for people at parties who refuse to sing at their turn.
Hert Heart
Hertz An Edinburgh football team.
Het Hot.
Hev Hive. Where bees live
Hevz M Hives. Heatspots.
Hid Had. **Alt: Hud.**
Hidni Had not. **Alt: Hudnay. Hidnay.**
Hing Hang.
Hingin Hanging
Hiv Have. **Alt: Hae.**
Hivee Heavy. **Pr:** as in mivvi.

Hivin M: Heaven. Having. **Alt: Hae-in.**
Hivnay Have not. **Alt: Hivni. Huvnay.**
Hivni Have not. **Alt: Huvnay. Huvni.**
Hiy Hay.
Hiyst Hoist.
Hiystee To give another person a lift up. **Alt: Scoutsir.**
Hiz Has
Hiznay Has not. **Alt: Hizni.**
Hizni Has not. **Alt: Hiznay**
Hoarn Horn.
Hoojimi Word used to describe something that is unknown or not remembered.
Hoor Word of rural origin. A woman of low morals.
Hoose House.
Hotties Hot shower and Bath section at Swimming baths.
Howk Dig.
Howked Dug
Howkin Digging
Howkir Used with **Tah-ay.**
Person who goes to annual Potato harvest.
Hucky-duck Now extinct boys street game.
Hud M Hold. Had. **Alt: Hid**
Hudd To take a hold of.

Huddik Haddock. Very good with chips.
Huddin Holding.
Hudnay Had not. **Alt: Hidni.**
Hudni Had not. **Alt: Hidni. Hudnay.**
Hull Hill. Not the city.
Hummin Of bad odour.
Humphy Hunchback.
Hundir The number on Hundred
Hundirwecht Hundredweight.
Hundirz Multiples of one Hundred.
Hung-iry Hungry **Pr:** as in hung. Generally only used to describe a money grabbing person. **ie. Hung- iry** Mary, a Dundee publican 1950s-70s.
Hunky Handkerchief. Not common in Dundee.
Hunt Haunt.
Huntit M Haunted. Description of lucky person.
Hup Hip
Hupnae Pre decimal Halfpence.
Hupnosis Hypnosis.
Hur Her.
Hurl To be transported. **eg.** "I got a **Hurl** in my Uncle's car".
Hurz Possessive form of Her
Hut Hit. Only as in smack. **ie.** The ball **Hut** me in the teeth.
Huv Have. **Alt: Hiv, Hae**
Huvna I have not.
Huvnay Alt: Have not. **Alt: Hivni. Huvni. Hivnay**
Huvni Have not. **Alt: Hivni. Huvnay. Hivnay**

I

i M: I. **Pr:** i as in lit. **eg.** i didn't do it. **Alt: eh.** Of. **eg.** A lot i rubbish. To. **eg**Are you going i the match tomorrow.
Iboot About.
Ibrode Abroad.
Iccoont Account.
Icoardee-in Accordian. What Jimmy Shand played.
Idvez Advise.
Ifore Before. **Alt: Afore.**
Ihent Behind. **Alt: Ahent.**
ILane Alone. **Alt: alane.**
Ile Oil.
Ilev Alive. **Alt: Alehv**
Ill I will. **Alt: Ull.**
Iloa Below. **Alt: Aloa.**
Im M I am. Him
Inah As well. **Alt: Ana**

Ingin Onion. **Pr: Ing** as in fling.
Inginz Plural of Onions.
Inglish English. **Pr: Ing** as in fling.
Inithir Another.
Inkwer Inquire.
Intae Into. **Alt: Inti**
Inti Into. **Alt: Intae**
Ipert Apart
Ippleh Apply
Ir Are. **Ir** you going to the pub. Her. ie. Is that **ir** coat in the lobby.
Iredee **Alt:** Already

Ingin Johnnys. Men who cycled all the way from France and sold Inginz from door to door.

Irnay Are not. Alt: Irni.
Irni Are not. Alt: Irnay
Irsell Herself.
isehlum Asylum

iside Aside
ithir Other.
Itween Between. **Alt: Atween**.
Ivir Ever.
Ivree Every.
Iwah Away **Alt: Awa.**
Iwahk Awake. **Alt: Awak.**
Iy Always. **Pr:** as in tide.
Iz M: Is. Sometimes used in place of Me. **eg** 'he asked iz to go to the pub with him'.
Iznae Is not. **Alt: Izni**
Izni Is not. **Alt: Iznae**

J

Jah Jaw.
Jait What Dundee is made of.
Jandaiz Jaundice. Used mainly to describe getting to Close to a person or object that is very dirty. **eg:** that wid gee yi the **Jandaiz**".
Jaz Plural of Jaw. See **Jah**. A film about a shark.
Jeckit Jacket.
Jek Familiar for John.
Jeloos Near extinct word meaning Comprehend or understand.
Jerjy Jersey, the item of clothing, not the place.
Jev Dance popular with Teddy boys..

Jevin The act of doing the Jive.
Jevir Person who does the Jive
Jiggin Dancehall.
Jile Jail.
Jileh July.
Jine Join.
Jine-ir Joiner.
Jined Joined
Jisnoo Just now.
Jist Just.
Jiste Joist.
Jistifeh Justify
Jiynt Joint
Jiynts Joints
Joab Job.
Joarj George.
Joeyz St Josephs. A Dundee school.
Johnyz St Johns. A Dundee school.
Joo Do you. **eg**. "**Joo** know What time it is?".

K

Kale Type of soup.
Kaz Cause
Kazd Caused
Kazin Causing. **Eg**: 'He is
always k**azin** trouble'.
Keech Faeces. Generally Only used to describe something that
is considered rubbish. **eg**. "You are talking a lot of **Keech**".

Keek Peek.
Keekin Peeking
Keekir Black eye.
Kerried Carried. **Alt: Kertit.**
Kerry Carry
Kerry-in Carrying.
Kert Cart.
Kertin Carrying.
Kertit Carried.
Kid Could.
Kidnae Could not. **Alt: Kidni.**
Kidni Could not. **Alt: Kidnae.**
Kin Can.
Kippy-up Co-habitee. One of an unmarried co-habiting couple.
Kirkahdee Kirkaldy.
Kirrie Kirriemuir. Another place where **Choochtirs** live. See **Choochtir** and **Farfir**. **Kirriemair** Kirriemuir. Alt to **Kirrie**
Kribee Kerb. Edging stones along roadside. Also **Kribee** Mixture, a rolling tobacco made from discarded
cigarette ends. See **Dowpee**.
Kwahrtir Quarter
Kwary Quarry
Kweh-it Quiet.

1300 BC Pharoah Amenhotep IV and his Kippy-up Nefertiti.

L

Lade Lead, the metal.
Lah **M** Hill in the middle of Dundee. See also **Hull**. Also used to describe Law, but only when threatening to get the police. See **Boabeez**.
Lampy Lamp post.
Lan Lawn.
Landry Laundry.
Lang Long.
Langirs Long trousers.
Larry Lorry.
Lavee Toilet.
Lavees Plural of Toilet.
Layn Lean. As in to lean on something, not as in meat.
Laynin Leaning.
Layv Leave. To depart, not a soldiers holiday.
Layvees Leftovers. Unheard of in Dundee households.
Layvin Leaving.
Lebry Library.
Leddir Ladder.

Jacob had a Leddir

Lee Lie. Falsehood. **Alt: Leh.** Word more of choochtir origin.
Lee-ir Person who tells falsehoods. **Alt: Leh-ir.**
Lee-in Lying
Leez Multiple falsehoods.
Alt: Lehz.
Leh **M** Lie. The horizontal position. Tell falsehoods. A singular falsehood. Also used in conjunction with **Lang** to describe staying in bed late in the mornings. eg: A **Lang Leh.**

Leh-in M The act of telling falsehoods. Being in the horizontal position.
Lehr Person who tells falsehoods, not person in horizontal position.
Leh-ir Letter
Lehsins Licence.
Len M Loan. **ie.** A loan of money. To take advantage of someone.
Lev Live. **Pr:** as in hive.
Lez M Multiple falsehoods. Verb of person in the horizontal position. "He just **Lez** in his bed all day". Person who tells a lot of falsehoods on a regular basis.**eg:** "She just **Lez** all the time". **Alt: Leez.** Also short for male Person named Leslie.
Licht M Light. **Pr ch** asin loch. To set something on fire. To light a cigarette. **eg.** " Could I have a **Licht** Please". Bright. The weight of an object.
Lichty To describe something as bright. **eg.** " It is very **Lichty** the night".
Linolyum Linoleum.
Lit Let.
Loabee Passageway behind front door in houses. Sometimes used in conjunction with **Dossir** and **Press. eg: Loabee dossir.** A person of lazy and intemperate habits. The **Loabee Press.** A large built in cupboard in the **Loabee.** See **Dossir** and **Press.**
Loag Log.
Lowp Jump.
Lowpin M Jumping. Terrible. **eg.** "That pint was **Lowpin**".
Luft Lift.
Luftit M Lifted. Arrested **eg.** 'I got **luftit** for being drunk'.
Lug Ear.
Luggee Small bucket used at raspberry picking. Usually tied round waist with a tie or snake belt.
Lugz Ears.
Luj M Lodge. As in Masonic lodge. To lodge acomplaint.
Lum Chimney
Lup M Lip. Being cheeky. **eg.** "Don't you give me any of your **Lup**, my lad".

M

Mahkin Making.
Maik Pre decimal Halfpence.
Mair More
Maist Most

Mait M Meat. Food in general.
Mak Make.
Manky Dirty.
Marri Marrow. Found inside bones. Not the vegetable.
Meelee M Melee. A type of pudding made with oatmeal. In Dundee, this is deep fried in batter and referred to as a White Pudding. Also a fight involving several persons.**Meenit** Minute. The unit of time, not as in small.
Meenits Minutes.
Meh My.
Meninjetis Meningitis.
Mennir Manner.
Mennirz Manners.
Mentull Mental.

King George III was totally Mentull

Merried Married.
Merrij Marriage.

Merry Marry.
Mestir Master.
Mibee Maybe.
Micht Might.
Michty Mighty.
Midden M: Walled off area at back of tenements where household waste was put before bins introduced. Used to describe any sort of dirty place, or to describe a dirty person.
Mijee Midge.
Mijeez Plural of Midge.
Miykeez St Michaels. A Dundee school.
Min Word of **Choochtir** origin. Used as a greeting or to attract a person's attention. eg. "Hey **Min**, have you got a light". See **Choochtir**.
Mind Remember.
Mindin Remembering.
Mingin Dirty.
Mink Person of dirty and slovenly habits. **Alt: Minkir.**
Minkir Alt: **Mink**.
Minter Red face Embarrassment
Misse-i Messiah.
Misell Myself.
Mithir Mother.
Miy The month of May. Not a woman named May.
Moa-ir Motor.
Moarn Tomorrow. Always prefixed with

267

"The".
Moarnin Morning.
Mooch Scrounge.
Mooched Past tense of Scrounge.
Moochin Act of to Scrounge.
Moochir. Scrounger.
Mock chop Food item in shape of pork chop. Unique to Dundee chip shops. Ingredients and origin unknown and remain a mystery.
Moose Mouse.
Mooth Mouth.
Moothee Mouthorgan.
Moothoargin Mouthorgan.
Mulk M Milk.
Mull Mill. As in where Jute is processed. **eg:** Mull of Kintyre, where Paul McCartney worked.
Mump Moan
Mumpin Moaning
Mup I am up. Usual answer to **Yup**. See **Yup**.
My Mother.

N

N And.
Nab **M** Catch. As in to catch a neer do well who has committed some skulduggery.An attractive girl. To make love to.
Nabbed Past tense of **Nab**. **eg:** "He stole a bike, but the police **Nabbed** him". The act of making love.
Nabbin M Catching. Making love to.
Nablir Person who is very good at picking berries at the annual harvest. Usually women and minks.
Nae No.
Naebdee Nobody.
Naewhar Nowhere.
Nah No.
Nait Neat. Generally used as a statement regarding a persons intentions.**eg**: If a person was asked if they were going to the pub, they might reply. "**Nait** I am".
Naitired Natured. As in a Persons temperament. Often used in conjunction with **Gaid** or **Ull**. **Eg**. "He is an **Ull Naitered** old person".
Nane None
Naykit Naked.
Neckit Necked. Generally only used in conjunction with the word "Hard". Used to describe a person who takesrisks for gain.
Neep M. Turnip. The Head. See **Haid**.
Neepsville Forfar. See

268

Farfir.
Neepwallipir M: Native of Forfar. **Choochtir.** A person who works or resides in the countryside.
Nerry   Narrow.
Nicht   Night.

Neepsville Athletic FC Team photo 2013.

Nippir   Part smoked cigarette that has been put out with the intention of smoking later.
Nippit   Tight. As in Tight fitting. eg. " These shoes are a bit **Nippit**".
Alt: Ticht.
No   Not.
Nock   Steal.
Nocked   Stolen.**eg:** I left My cigarettes on the table and somebody **Nocked** them.
Nockin   Stealing. The act of to Nock.
Noo   Now.
Nood   Nude.

Nood book   Book with pictures of naked women.
Nooz   News.
Noozpaipir   M: Newspaper. Toilet paper.
Nup   M. Nip. A measure of whisky. More of **Choochtir** origin than Dundee
Nut   No. Not.
Nu-hin   Nothing.

Nood book

O

Oardir   Order.
Oargin   Organ.
Oarinj   Orange.
Oary   To speak in a rough manner
Oavin   Oven.
Oh   Of. **Alt: i**
Ony   Any
Oor   M   Our. Hour. May cause confusion with certain phrases. **eg**. "We

will have to wait an **Oor** for **Oor** bus".
Oorz M Ours. Hours.
Oot Out. Also the sound a Cockney owl makes.
Owir Over.
Oxtir The armpit.

P

Pah M Paw. **ie.** A cat's Paw. To touch profusely.
Pahd Pawed.
Pah-in Pawing
Pahnd M Pawned. Smashed.
Pair Poor.
Pan M Pawn. Place where loans are given. To smash. **eg.**"I am going to **Pan** that window in".
Pattyz St Patricks. A Dundee school.
Peece Sandwich. Famous Dundee sandwiches inc: broon sas, condensed mulk, sugar, lemon curd.
Peece-n Used to describe contents of sandwich **ie.** A **Peece-n** jam/cheese/sas
Peek Scrap metals such as lead, brass and copper.
Peelee wahly White faced, Ashen.
Peel Pill
Peelz Pills.
Peen Pin.
Peh Pie. Nuf said!

Pehlit Pilot. Not Pontius.
Pendee Narrow passageway between buildings.
Pent Paint.
Pentin The act of painting, or a picture composed of paint.
Pentir Person who Paints.
Pentit Painted.
Pert Part.
Pertin parting.
Pertit Parted.
Perty Party.
Pez Pies. Eaten profusely in Dundee. Real **Pez** are filled with minced mutton. Other fillings available, ie. steak, chicken, macaroni, curry, but not considered real **Pez**. Fillings along with mutton inc: bean, tattie, tattie and bean, pea. Also commonly eaten on a roll.
Pictirs Cinema. Alt: **Show.**
Pike To spy on furtively.
Pike-in The act of spying on furtively.
Piker Person who spies on furtively.
Piler Boys cart made out of wood and old pram wheels.
Pinner Now extinct boys game.
Pinsil Pencil.

Piy Pay.
Piyd Past tense of pay
Piy-in Paying.
Piyzin Poison
Piyzined Poisoned.
Plaze Please.
Plazed Pleased.
Plaze-in Pleasing.
Pleh Ply.
Plehwid Plywood.
Plen **M** Plain. Generally used with **Brade.**
Plerz Pliers.
Plestir **M** Plaster. The substance applied to walls. General term for person who messes around.
Plestired Plastered.
Plestirin Plastering, both to apply the substance to walls, and to mess around.
Plestirir. Plasterer. Person who applies plaster to walls.
Pletty Verandahs used for access to houses in Tenements
Ploo Plough. Also a Dundee pub till 1982. See also:
Neepsville, Choochter.
Ploo-in Ploughing.
Ploomin Person who ploughs, see **Choochtir.**
Plook Singlular Acne.
Plookee Description of face which has multiple **Plooks**

Typical 1950s Dundee Pletty

Plunderin Pinching tree fruit
Plunk Truancy.
Plunked Truanted
Plunkin Truanting
Plunkir Truant.
Pochil To cheat out of money. **Pr**: ch as in loch.
Pochils Money obtained by deception.
Pochlin The act of to **Pochil**
Poor Pour.
Poorin Pouring. **ie**. It is **Poorin** of rain
Poze Hide
Pozed Hid.
Pozee-hole Secret place for hiding things
Press Large built in cupboard.
Prevít Private.
Prez **M** Prize. Prise.
Puhl Pull.
Puhlae Pillow.
Puhlishee Long looped rope running between building and tall wooden

pole at back of tenements. Meant for hanging washing on.
Pund Pound. The unit of weight. Not the currency denomination.
Pus The face.
Pusy To do something which is considered unnecessary. A person who is a nuisance.
Pusy-in The act of to **Pusy**.
Pusyed Past tense of pusy-in. **eg:** He **Pusyed** about in the garden all day.
Pyuchy Person of rural origin. **Pr: ch** as in loch **Alt: Choochtir.**

R

Ra Raw. Not the Egyptian sun god.
Rade Red
Ragit Ragged.
Rake Look for.
Rakin Looking for.
Rammy Stramash.
Reeleefoe Children's game similar to hide and seek, but where captives can get free if a player gets to block unseen and shouts **Reeleefoe.**
Reelez Realize. **Alt: Rilez**
Ren Rain.
Rennin Raining
Renned Rained
Renz Rains ie. I am not going out if it **Renz**
Rez Rise. **Alt: Riyz.**
Rezin Rising.
Richt Right.
Ridee Ready.
Rilez Realize **Alt: Reelehz**
Rither Rather.
Riyz Rise. **Alt: Rez.**
Rocky Rockwell. A Dundee school.
Roond Round.
Roondirz Game similar to baseball.
Row Roll. As in a bread roll.
Pr: As in row, to quarrel.

S

Sad Sawed.
Sade Said
Saffy Its awful, that's awful, is awful.
Saft Soft.
Safty A weak person.
Sah M. Saw. Both to see, and the cutting tool.
Sah-in The act of sawing a piece of wood.
Sah-yir Tradesman who saws timber by mechanical means.
Sain Soon
Sair Sore.
Sait Seat.

Sang Song. May cause confusion in certain circumstances. **eg**. "I sang a **Sang**".
Sanny Gymn shoe. Plimsoles.
Sannies Plural of **Sanny**. Plimsoles. **Sannies** came in two distinct styles, laced and slip-ons, and came in three colours, black, white and brown. Along with Wellingtons, they were standard year round footwear for children in Dundee till the 1960s, when replaced by plastic sandals.
Santy Santa, as in Santa Claus. **Santy Claz**
Sark Shirt.
Sas Sauce. Comes in two
forms: broon or tamati
Sasij Sausage.
Sassir Saucer. Generally
only used by posh fowk, or to feed cats with.
Sat Salt.
Scoosh M: Squirt. **Alt: Scoot.** Lemonade.
Scoot Squirt. **Alt: Scoosh**
Scoo-ee hoy Horse drawn machine that squirted water on to streets during summer.
Scoutsir Means of giving a person a leg up. See **Hiystee**.
Scrammy Money thrown to children at weddings.
Scubee Covered in scabs.
Scubee touch A children's game similar to tig. Disease. Infected people had to live in "colonies".
Scuttir M: To mess around. **Alt: Pusy. Plestir. Footir.** also person who **Scuttirs. eg:** He is a **Scuttir**
Scuttired Past tense of **Scuttir.**
Scuttirin Alt: Pusy-in. Plestirin. Footirin.
Seek Sick.
Seevin Seven.
Seevinteen Seventeen..
Seevinth Seventh.
Seevinty Seevinty.
Seh Sigh.
Seh-ins Science.
Sek Sack. Both a bag and dismissal from a job.
Selins Silence.
Selt Sold.
Seh-irday Saturday
Sez M Size. Says.
Sha Shaw
SHaidee Shadow.
Shair Sure.
Shairly Surely.
Sheh Shy
Shi She
Shill She will.

273

Shillno She will not.
Shin M: Shoes. Word of **Choochtir** origin. Is she in.
Shitehoose M: Generally only used to describe a nasty person. Also word for toilet.
Shithir Shoulder.
Shithiree To carry someone on the shoulders
Shiveree Shivery. Occasionally used with Bite eg: **Shiveree** bite. Snack eaten after visit to swimming baths.
Shiytee Toilet. **Alt: Lavee, Chanty.**
Shiz She is.
Shizni She is not. **Alt: Shizno**
Shizno She is not. **Alt: Shizni**
Shoart Short
Shoartirs Short trousers.
Shoor Shower.
Shoorz M: Showers. It is yours.
Shot Borrow. **eg:** could I have a **shot** of your bicycle.
Shotty Borrow. **Alt: Shot.**
Show Cinema. Show Jumping, getting on a Horse and getting it to jump over the Regal, Royalty etc.

Denis Healy. Chancellor of Exchequer. Got a Shot/Len of £28 billion from the IMF in 1978.

Shuft M: Shift. To move something. A work period. **eg:** the night Shuft. Changing clothes.
Shufted M Past tense of Shift. To change clothes.
Shuftir Shifter. A person employed in the jute trade.
Sicht. Sight.
Simmit Vest.
Sined Rinse. **Pr:** same as signed.
Singil Single. **Pr** as in fling.
Sipleh Supply.
Siprez Surprise.
Siroond Surround.
Siroondit Surrounded.
Sirvev Survive.
Skale School
Skeh Sky. You get **Peh** in the **Skeh** when you

Deh.
Skell Spill.
Skelp To hit. **Alt: Skite. Hut.**
Skelped Past tense of Hit.
Skelt Spilt.
Skite To hit. Alt: **Skelp**
Skitters Dioarhaea
Skwad Squad.
Skwash Squash
Skwashir Squasher. Ice cream slider with a chocolate snowball.
Skwat Squat.
Skwatir Person who quats,as in empty houses.
Skweeb Squib. Firework
Slabir Person who is sloppy with food. Evident by traces on face and clothes.
Slabired Sloppy with food.
Slabiree Description of a person who is sloppy with food ie. **Slabiree** Alec. A big fat **Booabee** who worked on east end beat in 1950s. Name came about through his face and tunic always being covered in traces of cake etc
Slabirin Being messy with food.
Sleekit Sly. See **Fle**.
Slup Slip.
Slupped Slipped.
Sluppy Slippy

The Chinese Invented Squeebs

Sma Small.
Smert Smart.
Sna Snow
Snaba M Snowball. Also a term of endearnment.
Snad Snowed
Sna-in Snowing
Snaz Snows.
Snoe Is not.
Snottir Nasal mucous.
Soajir Soldier.
Soart Sort.
Sook Suck.
Sooked Sucked.
Sookin Sucking
Sookir Used with **Dabbir**. **i Sookir n i Dabbir,** a now extinct childrens toy used for lifting paving slabs.
Soond Sound.
Soondz Plural of sound.
Soor Sour.
Sooth South. Not used to describe the direction. Only used to describe South

Road, a street in Dundee.
Sosh The Cooperative Society.
Sowil Soul. **Pr:** as in female pig. Generally only used with **Pair** to describe person who is having a hard time ie. A **Pair Sowil**
Spammy The act of moving from one high structure to another slightly higher structure by jumping, but landing at waist level using the hands to alight on to the higher structure.
Spane Spoon.
Spayvir Opening at front of trousers, either zipped or buttoned.
Spechul Special.
Speh spy.
Spew Vomit.
Spile Spoil.
Splut Split. Used with **Haid** to describe cut on head
Splutin The act of to Split. Used to describe headache.
Spookee Only used with Meeting to describe a Séance.
Spull Spill. **Alt: Skell.**
Spult Spilt. **Alt: Skelt.**
Spultir Overripe fruit. Usedby children to Play **Scubee** touch.

Sput Spit **Alt: Gochil.**

A Spookee meeting

Sputtin Spitting **Alt: Gochlin.**
Stahl Stall. Only used to describe a market stall.
Stail Steal.
Steer Stir.
Steh Sty. Stye. Both an eye infection and where pigs live.
Spyugee Sparrow. **Pr: g** as in goat.

Edith Piaf was known as The Little Spyugee.

Squeeb Firework.
Stahl Stall. Only used to describe a market stall.
Stail Steal.
Steer Stir.
Steh Sty. Stye. Both an eye infection and where pigs live.
Sterv Starve
Stervin Starving.
Stewpit Stupid.
Stick Stand. Used to describe a person that is not liked. **eg**. "I cannot **Stick** that person".
Stiy Stay.
Stiyed Stayed.
Stiy-in Staying.
Stiyz. Girdle women wear under clothes.
Stoabee Area of Dundee and a school.
Stoor Combination of dust, carpet fibres and hair sticking together inlumps. Usually found below beds.
Stoot Stout. As in a persons build. Not the drink.
Stott Bounce.
Stottid Bounced
Stottin Bouncing.
Stottir Something very good. good looking girl.
Stra Straw.
Strazirs Strawberries.
Strecht Straight.
Streetch Stretch
Stripit Striped.
Strup Strip.

Stull Still.
Swahlay Swallow. Not The bird.
Swahp Swap.
Swahrm Swarm.
Sweem Swim.
Sweemin **M:** The act of to swim.
Sweeng Swing.
Sweered Scared
Sweetee Sweet. As in confectionary.
Swick Cheat. **Alt: Chait.** Both the person and the act.
Swicked Cheated.
Swickin Cheating.
Swite Sweat.

T

Tah-ay Potato.
Tah-ayz Potatoes.
Tak Take.
Takin Taking.
Tal Tall.
Tap **M** Top. To borrow money.
Tappin Borrowing money.
Tay **M** Toe. To.
Taze Toes.
Teckil Tackle.
Teh Tie.
Telt Told.
Ter Tyre.
Terd Tired.
Terifeh Terrify.
Terifed Terrified.

Tert Tart.
Tez Ties.
Thae These.
Therty Thirty.
Thurteen Thirteen.
Thigithir Together.
Thin Than. **Pr: Th** same as in than
Thir They are.
Thirz There is.
Thoarn Thorn.
Thoarnz Thorns.
Thocht Thought.
Thoosint Thousand.
Thoosints Thousands.
Thra Strangle.
Thran Stubborn.
Threed Thread.
Thrupnae Three pence coin in pre decimal currency.
Thum Them.

A crown of Thoarnz, as worn by Jesus at the last supper.

Thurd Third
Ti To. **Alt: Tae**
Ticht Tight. **PR:** ch as in loch.

Tick Credit. As in a loan.
Ticky Unit of measurement.
Tike Mattress
Tink Travelling person. **Alt:**
Mink, Minker, Tinky.
Also used to describe a dirty person.
Tinky Alt: Tink.
Mink. Minker
Timati Tomato.
Timatiz Tomatoes.
Tiy The river Tay. **Pr:** same as tide.
Toaly A singular piece of faeces.
Toarn Torn.
Tool Towel
Toon Town.
Toothik Toothache.
Tow Tow. **Pr:** as in how.
Trachil Struggle
Trachiled Struggling.
Trait Treat.
Traitin Treating
Traitit Treated
Tre Try
Tred Tried.
Tre-in Trying.
Troot Trout.
Troozirz Trousers. **Alt: Breeks**
Tub Football tube.
Tugee Hair that comb wont go through.
Tull Till. Not Till used in shops.

Tully Local Dundee newspaper.
Twa Two.

U

Ull **M** I will. **Alt: Ehl.** Ill
Um I am. **Alt: Ehl**
Unce Ounce.

V

Valt Vault.
Vebrait Vibrate.
Velin Violin.
Velins **M**: both the plural of violin and violence.
Velint Violent.

W

Wa Wall
Wabil Wobble.
Wabit Tired
Wablee Wobbly.
Wadil Waddle.
Wah-ir Water
Wah-iry Watery.
Wahk **M**: Walk. Wake.
Wahked Walked. Waked.
Wahkin **M**: Walking Waking.
Wahkined Wakened.

Hadrians Wa, built by the Picts to keep the Romans out.

Wahkir Person named Walker.
Wahlip Wallop
Wahlit Wallet
Wahltz Waltz
Wahltzirs Waltzers. As in a ride at the carnival.
Wahnd Wand. Magic, like Sooty.
Wahndir Wander.
Wahndirin Wandering.
Wahndirir Wandirir. As in the Rock and Roll song by Dion.
Wahnt Want.
Wahnti Wanted
Wahr War
Wahrd Ward.
Wahrdin Warden.
Wahrdrobe Wardrobe.
Wahrm Warm.
Wahrn warn.
Wahry-ir Warrior.
Wahsh Wash.
Wahshae Washhouse.
Wahshir Washer.

Wahsp   Wasp.
Wahtch   Watch.
Wahty   Familiar for Walter.
Wecht   Weight.
Wee   **M** Small. With.
Weel   Well. Not the water tap on sink.
Weel-aff   Rich
Weeleewag   Small mischievous creature used to frighten children.
Weemin   Women.
Weeng   Wing.
Weet   Wet.
Weh   Way. **Alt: wiy**
Well   Water tap on sink
Wer   Wire.
Werlis   Radio.
Wez   **M** Ways. Wise
Wha   Who.
Whamee   Who me? Not a member of a red Indian tribe.
Whar   Where.
Wharaboots   Whereabouts
Wharz   Where is/are.
Whaz   **M** Who is. **eg: Whaz** that at the door?' Whose. **eg: 'Whaz** pint is that?'
Wheesht   To tell to be quiet.
Whut   What.
Whutfield   How **Choochtirs** say Whitfield.
Wi   **Alt: Wee M.** We. With.
Wid   **M** Wood. Would.

Widni   Would not.
Wifey   Woman.
Windee   Window.
Winnae   Wont.
Alt:Winni
Winni   Wont **Alt: Winnae**
Wir   **M** We are. Our.
Wiste   **M:** Waste. Waist.
Withir   Weather.
Wiv   We have.
Wiy   Way. Weigh.
Wiy-ir   Wire. **Alt** to **Wer.**
Wiyz   **M.** Wise. Ways. Weighs.
Wiz   Was.
Wiznae   Was not **Alt: Wizni**
Wizni   Was not. **Alt: Wiznae**
Wulk   Whelk.
Wull   Will. Not as in Last Will and Testament.
Wullnae   Will not. **Alt: Wullni.**
Wullni   Will not.
Wumin   Woman.

X

X   Belonging to Alexander. See **Eck**

Y

Yaird Yard.
Yaistirday Yesterday. A song by the Beatles and Daffy Duck.
Yase Use. As in, "Is this any **Yase** to you" **Yaze** Use. As in "I'll **Yaze** the shears to cut the grass"
Yaze-in Using.
Yazed Used.
Yasefil Useful
Yan Yawn.
Yelli Yellow.
Yi You.
Yid You would.
Yin Are you in.
Yiniy-it Dundee United.
Yir **M.** You are. Your.
Yirni You are not. **Alt: Yirnoa** Y ou are not. **Alt: Yirni**
Yirsell Yourself.
Yit Yet.
Yiz Plural of You. **ie** are **Yiz** going to the match?
Yooz **Alt: Yiz**
Yup Are you out of bed. Usual reply being **Mup.**

Z

Zat Is that
Zit Is it

That's ah fowks!

Made in the USA
Charleston, SC
01 May 2014